D1453990

Rolling in Dough

Rolling in Dough

Lessons I Learned in a Doughnut Shop

Glenn G. Sparks

White River Press
Amherst, Massachusetts

First published 2011
Update published 2018

White River Press
PO Box 3561
Amherst, MA 01004
www.whiteriverpress.com

ISBN: 978-1-935052-12-8

Library of Congress Cataloging-in-Publication Data

Sparks, Glenn Grayson.
Rolling in dough : lessons I learned in a doughnut shop / Glenn G. Sparks.
    p. cm.
ISBN 978-1-935052-12-8 (pbk. : alk. paper) -- ISBN 978-1-935052-41-8 (ebook)
1. Sparks, Glenn Grayson. 2. Bakeries--United States.
3. Doughnuts. 4. Small business--Management.
5. Entrepreneurship. I. Title.
HD9058.P372S63 2011
658--dc22
                    2011007544

This book is dedicated to my parents,
Calvin and Betty Sparks. All they ever
wanted for their family was our happiness
and for us to be together.

Acknowledgments

As this book becomes a reality, I owe a great debt to so many people. My mother, Betty, and my father, Calvin, took the incredible risk of changing careers when I was young in order to make my life better. Their sharp memories made writing this book much easier than it would have been if I had been forced to rely only on my personal recollections. Their love and devotion to their family was always certain. Without them, of course, this book would not have happened. And without my own family, the book would not have happened either. To my wife, Cheri (Dr. Cheri), and my three grown children, David, Erin, and Jordan, I can only say thank you. If I started to list the ways in which they have loved and supported me through this project, I'd still be writing. My three brothers, Dale, Wayne, and Garry provided many of the memories and stories that helped me put the book together. The four of us have always known that our experience as doughnut boys was not typical of the way middle-class boys grew up in America in the 1950s and 1960s.

I am also blessed with several friends who I know care about my welfare. Mike Bergmann, Em Griffin, John Greene, Will Miller, Bob Ogles, and Stuart Robertson have each inspired this project in different ways. I truly believe that no man could have a finer set of friends.

The idea to write this book took root years ago, even while my family continued to run the doughnut business. My wife, Cheri, kept the idea alive in discussions from time to time as we reflected on the things we wanted to accomplish. But the inspiring moment that finally motivated me to action happened when I least expected it.

Each year, I take one weekend and travel to St. Louis with a few other professors to watch a weekend baseball series. I love baseball. While we were on the road, conversation turned to our childhoods and I ended up sharing some of the experiences from my life in the doughnut shop. That evening, Saturday, June 6, 1998, my close friend John Greene and I went out to have a beer and nachos after a 14-inning game between the Cardinals and Giants. The Cards lost 5-4. Our disappointment at the fact that Mark McGwire had not hit another home run probably motivated us to add a little pleasure to the trip and dine out, even though the hour was already late. As we munched nachos, John returned to our earlier conversations from the ride to St. Louis and encouraged me to bring this project into focus. It was a defining moment. Who knows what would have happened if McGwire had homered and we had gone right back to the hotel and gone to sleep? This book might still be a faint vision in my mind.

So I give a special thanks to John and to my other baseball buddies (Hank Scheele, Dan Wilcox, Steve Wilson and Ralph Webb) who seemed to derive some pleasure from hearing my stories about doughnuts. I'm also grateful to Mark McGwire for not hitting one of his record-shattering 70 home runs that day. After settling on the idea of writing the book, my friend Will Miller gave me additional inspiration for using the raw material as the basis for a corporate speech. That fantasy helped motivate me to write even though I have yet to deliver any speeches on the content.

I also need to thank my friend and colleague George Stevens, who read through the manuscript at least twice and asked questions, offered advice, and provided great suggestions to make the book better. Several other people read at least one of the preliminary drafts and provided helpful reactions—including Conrad Wilcox, Rob Cooper, Dennis Dunn, Bob Ogles, and Patrice Buzzanell. My years as a writer of scholarly journal articles, and a text book for undergraduate students helped to convince me of the value of a great copy editor. I was fortunate to have Robyn Tellefsen for that task. I also am grateful to Howard Sypher, head of the Department of Communication at Purdue University. I've served as associate head of the department for most of the years that I've worked on this project. Howard encouraged me to bring this project to fruition and helped provide the supportive climate that most professors only dream about.

By the time this book appears in print, it will be close to 13 years since I was inspired to write it. During that time, my parents both passed away—but not before they had read a draft of the manuscript. In retrospect, I think I delayed moving ahead with the project at full speed because I sensed some ambivalence on the part of my parents, particularly my father. While he was proud of the fact that he had run a successful business for 20 years, he also had many regrets about the way certain things turned out and he tended to ruminate about those regrets. I never wanted the publication of this volume to trigger a new round of negative ruminations for him.

I have to thank my wife, Cheri, once again for helping keep the fire on this project alive once it was ignited. This past summer, we celebrated 35 years of marriage together. May there be many more.

Glenn Sparks
Spring 2011

Foreword

I wrote this book mainly because of my sense that people seemed to be intrigued, entertained, and even fascinated when they heard me tell of the various things that happened during my family's experience running a doughnut shop. Nine of the 10 chapters of the book contain stories designed to illustrate a lesson learned along the way. If these tales prove useful for someone contemplating a family business, then I'll be thrilled. But in all honesty, the book's "lessons" are really just an organizing scheme that allowed me to tell the many stories that I have told over and over through the years to friends and members of my extended family.

In reflecting on the overall impression that one might have after reading the book, I realized that there is some danger inherent in putting together a collection of memories. The most colorful memories are not necessarily the ones that tend to place people in the most favorable light. If I have any misgiving about the content of the book it is that the collection of stories, taken as a whole, may fail to capture the extent to which I believe that both my father and mother were wonderful human beings. During the 20 years that they operated the doughnut shop, they were held in incredibly positive regard by virtually everyone who knew them well. My mother had a keen sense of appropriate social behavior. She smiled at people, always had a cheerful word, and believed that these behaviors were crucial to teach to me and my brothers. My father shared these values and brought curiosity, concern, and goodwill to all of his interactions with others. This caused everyone who talked with him to walk away with a feeling of importance and the knowledge that he cared about them.

My parents shared another great gift: they never let too much time pass before they laughed. They were able to find humor in the midst of the toughest circumstances. And if they couldn't find it on the surface, they wouldn't hesitate to dig down a few layers and manufacture it. My father was a bit of a ham and my mother supported and encouraged him to play that role. Fortunately for them—and for us—running a doughnut shop provided enough material to keep my brothers and me laughing all these years later. Whenever we get together, our conversation inevitably breaks into raucous delight as we recall some of the things that happened in the doughnut business. We owe our ability to laugh our way through life to the extraordinary character and personalities of our mother and father.

If you find yourself reading a story in the pages that follow and think that it doesn't reflect well on my parents, remember that they probably laughed at themselves for whatever limitation or failing one might perceive. And then they passed that laughter on to us. Nothing would make my folks happier than to think that someone else laughed at their life adventure years afterward. Any 20-year period in a family's life contains some sadness, and there are certainly struggles and sadness in some of the stories I tell. But I hope that on balance, I've managed to capture enough of the humor to balance the sadness. In any case, my parents were wonderful people. Hopefully, you'll reach that conclusion without my help. But the point is such an important one that I want to be explicit about it from the start.

Contents

Rolling in Dough

Chapter 1

Introduction: 8.5 Million Doughnuts Later

In the hot summer month of July when I was 11 years old, my father left a career in structural engineering and moved the family to another state to open a doughnut shop. It was a family business, in a manner of speaking. Every family member worked in the shop over the years, but some worked more than others. My parents worked the most. Between me and my three brothers (two older, one younger), we also contributed a significant number of hours to making the business run. But in terms of the labor provided by the four boys, I probably contributed the most. When I was 12, I literally begged my mother to teach me how to "finish" the doughnuts, for a wage of $1 per hour. It seemed to me like I had struck it rich. One of my older brothers (by only 22 months), Wayne, thought I was crazy. Who would want to work in a doughnut shop with their parents? In Wayne's case, he had at least 100 better things to do. Some of those things were illegal, like taking joyrides at night in my dad's car years before he was old enough to get a license. Eventually, Wayne's antics became so serious that my parents sent him away to military school for his last year of high school. This was not so much a decision as it was an act of desperation. Kids and small businesses present a real catch-22. Sometimes, kids can help make the business run. But frequently, their presence underscores a tough reality—there is little time to parent. When Wayne went away to military school, it meant that my parents had to rely on me even more to work in the doughnut shop. And for the most part, I didn't mind.

"Finishing" the doughnuts involved such things as coating them with sugar, crumbs, icing, whipped cream, or, whenever my dad got a creative insight, something exotic like tomato sauce or Cheese Whiz (a pizza doughnut). Of course, my dad's innovative ideas did not always result in success—like the time he got the notion to fly 10 kites that were all hooked together and arrayed in a huge triangle that resembled a bowling pin arrangement. He worked on that configuration for weeks. As I recall, he had collected the kites on multiple visits to a local Texaco gas station. Each kite displayed the Texaco logo and it was possible that my dad was hoping that his kite contraption would attract the attention of Texaco's marketers and result in some compensation. But when the time came to fly the kites, we could hardly get the formation out the front door. When we did, the individual kites instantly blew in 10 different directions and the structure fell apart.

I would put the pizza doughnut in the same category with the kites—a fleeting operation. But the fact that we had a pizza doughnut at all sheds light on my dad's personality. He was always looking for a new angle. If you had talked with him about the pizza doughnut, he would have taken issue with the notion that the venture was short-lived. Instead, he would have emphasized all of the labor we undertook to keep this doughnut in the product line. He often featured it on a daily special or tried to display it in a more prominent position in the display case. His memory differed from my own about how long we actually offered this novelty. I recall it as a temporary experiment that failed. My dad seemed to remember that the pizza doughnut was a mainstay after its introduction.

The best part of finishing the doughnuts was the chance to squirt jelly deep into the cavity of the yeast shell. The different flavors of jelly were stored in banana-yellow containers that, when needed, were lifted onto a shiny, silver-colored, electric pumping machine called a homogenette. After rolling the yeast shells in a large aluminum bin filled with granulated sugar, I would take two doughnuts, one in each hand, and stick them onto the two shiny posts that protruded from the yellow pumps. One quick thump on the "fill" button on the lower part of the homogenette would open the pump and, like magic, a pre-measured quantity of jelly would squirt into the doughnuts. A good doughnut finisher is one who can fill a tray of doughnuts (eight rows of nine doughnuts each) with speed, while simultaneously taking care not to squash them. Doughnuts are fragile when they're fresh, so even a good finisher loses a small percentage to mishandling. But squashed doughnuts don't look good and they don't sell well. In the end, the combination of speed and fragile handling required to finish doughnuts makes it a difficult job to master. There is a kind of artistic grace involved in finishing doughnuts well.

By the time I was 15 years old, I was convinced that I was the best doughnut finisher in the world. Today, the pattern of filling doughnuts with jelly is so deeply ingrained in my neural pathways that I am convinced I could return to the doughnut shop today and pick up right where I left off. Often, the last thing I did before I began my clean-up at the end of a shift was see how much jelly I could stuff into a doughnut without the doughnut shell exploding. Sometimes, when I hit it just right and had two doughnuts that felt like they were loaded with lead, I would sneak them into the appropriate tray in the display case. I always visualized someone biting into those doughnuts and having to cope with a virtual jelly explosion. My dad never knew I did this. It was a complete violation of the rules that my parents had so carefully taught me. Each doughnut was supposed to have just the right amount of jelly—no more, no less. Needless to say, my dad lost money on the "loaded" doughnuts. But some customers probably raved about how much jelly we put in and came back for more. I like to think that in terms of business, this little game may have made us as much money as it lost. But it probably didn't.

From Doughnuts to Dormitories

I left the doughnut shop to attend college in Illinois. I am now a professor of communication. When I introduce myself to students on the first day of class and try to learn their names, I encourage them to tell me something about themselves that is unique so I will remember them better. To give them an example of the sort of thing I want them to say, I decided to compute an estimate of the number of doughnuts that passed through my hands during the years that I worked as a doughnut finisher. My best estimate is eight-and-a-half million. This fact is now part of my identity. I am the professor who has handled nearly nine million doughnuts. I tend to think that this is somehow more significant than the number of research articles that I have published. And judging from my students' reactions, I am certain they feel the same way. Inevitably when I meet former students in local restaurants, they say nothing regarding the interesting research they learned about in my classes. Instead, they smile and say, "Hey, don't I remember you saying that you grew up in a doughnut shop and have handled millions of doughnuts?" After years of these interactions, I have learned to be proud of my history.

But being proud of my history is not the reason I decided to write this book. As I indicated in the foreword, many people encouraged me to write an account of the stories I often told in casual conversation. I also thought it would simply be fun to write this kind of book. I've spent the last 20 years writing research articles on the effects of the mass media. That's been fun too—but I suppose I wanted to try a different type of writing for a change of pace. Another reason to write about doughnuts has to do with my parents. Years ago, I talked with them about writing a book like this and I think they always wanted me to try. So I did.

A Word About Names

In reflecting on the doughnut shop, my intent isn't to drag up memories that disparage anyone. Nevertheless, if I've learned anything about communication as a result of my scholarly study in that field, I know that what some people perceive as colorful and amusing are the very same things that other people might find to be less than pleasant. Consequently, I've changed all names except for those of my family members. I've also scrupulously avoided iden- tifying the location of our store or the name of the fran- chise doughnut shop that we ran. I've also steered away from describing anyone's particular circumstances in such detail that it might be possible to discover that person's true identity.

I've done these things to minimize the chance that others might misconstrue anything in this book as a complaint about any individual or about the parent company. That's not my intent. My only motivation in talking about specific people or about the parent company is to convey our family experience as my family members and I remember it. No one in my family, including myself, holds any malice toward any person that I mention in the book or toward the parent company of our franchise. While some of my stories will clearly reflect tensions between my family, various individuals, and the company, such tensions were typical throughout the franchise industry at the time we operated our doughnut shop. And the experts often point out that the source of these tensions can be traced to the particular interaction of characters on both sides of the franchisee-franchisor relationship. I'm sure that's true. For the record, I still eat doughnuts. In fact, I enjoy an occasional visit to a doughnut shop and I feel grateful in many ways for the chance I had to work under the franchise name.

The Theme of the Book

Regardless of what station in life you happen to be in as you pick up this book, I hope the stories that unfold will at least be interesting to read. If you do happen to be entertaining the idea of going into business, the book has a major theme to keep in mind: **Before you go into business, do some research, then do some more research, and then, when you think you've done enough research, do some more research.** As will become evident, my family really could have benefited from several more months of research before deciding to go into business.

Don't just talk to people who tell you what you want to hear. Listen carefully to people who tell you things that tend to spoil your dream—they could be the most important people to spend time with. They might spare you from making costly mistakes in your efforts to realize your dream career.

If you have no plans to go into business, I hope that my reflections on running a doughnut shop will simply take you into a different world and prove to be an enjoyable read.

Chapter 2

Don't Go Into Business to Get More Time with the Kids

My earliest recollections of my dad's preoccupation with doughnuts go back long before he ever owned a doughnut shop, to about 1961 when I was 8 years old. My dad didn't like the 9-to-5 grind of his engineer's job, and he fantasized about having a source of income that could support the family at an even higher level, while simultaneously giving him more control over his schedule so he could spend more time with me and my three brothers. My oldest brother, Dale, delivered the evening newspaper during the week to earn a little spending money. But his grades in elementary school were suffering and my dad was looking for a way for Dale to earn money in less time. He had learned in a conversation with the son of his second cousin that *his* way of earning money was to have a doughnut route—in contrast to a paper route.

Several days later, a friend of my mom's came to the house to visit and just happened to be carrying a bag of warm powdered-sugar doughnuts. When my dad bit into one, all kinds of lightbulbs went on in his brain. Doughnut routes were the answer to life! It was all the inspiration he needed. If boys could be motivated by delivering newspapers for cash, then perhaps they could be motivated to deliver other things door-to-door—like doughnuts. Before we knew what was happening to our idyllic Saturday mornings watching

Sky King on TV or playing a neighborhood baseball game, my brothers and I were peddling doughnuts around the city.

Sunday Morning Doughnut Routes

Sunday mornings started early. We would rise at 4:30 a.m. and drive to a bakery in the downtown area. At the beginning, my brothers and I delivered one to two doughnuts as "free samples." Then, we went back to take orders for the coming week. Reflecting back on it, I sometimes wonder whether the people who received these free samples reacted the way I would if I received one at my house today. Maybe it was a different world back then. Maybe not. In any case, imagine yourself going to the front door on Sunday morning to retrieve the newspaper. As you open your door, you notice a small plastic bag hanging on the door handle. Inside the bag is a glazed doughnut and a small piece of paper instructing you where to call if you wanted a dozen doughnuts delivered next Sunday. Would you actually *eat* the doughnut in the bag? I think I might ask myself where this doughnut came from. Who delivered it? My paranoid side might wonder if someone was trying to poison me. I might think about all of the media warnings about Halloween candy and examine the doughnut to see if it had a razor blade in it. Maybe these questions and concerns just didn't occur to people back in 1962. Maybe the world was more like the one depicted in the movie *Pleasantville*. In any case, enough people phoned in orders to convince my dad that he was on to something big.

I remember four different kinds of doughnuts that formed the core of our business: glazed (we called them honey-dipped), Boston creame (custard filled with chocolate frosting), jelly-filled, and plain chocolate-frosted. By virtue of his age, Dale usually got to get up at 4:30 a.m. and accompanied my dad to the bakery to help load the doughnuts into our green Volkswagen Beetle. I'm not sure how my dad managed to convince Dale that this was actually a privilege. Shortly after their return from the bakery, Wayne and I were to be ready to hit the streets early and provide people with fresh doughnuts for their breakfast. We sold the doughnuts for about 60 cents per dozen. The profit margin was small. Eventually, we moved the operation to Saturday mornings because it was too difficult to finish our routes and get to church on time.

I have just a few vivid memories from these early days. Sometimes, in addition to the doughnuts that were preordered, my dad would order an extra 30 dozen (10 dozen each for me, Wayne, and Dale). We had to sell these doughnuts door-to-door with no preorders. There was something a little odd about ringing people's doorbells at 9 o'clock on a Saturday morning. For every person who had just sat down to breakfast and was delighted to have doughnuts presented for sale at the front door, there must have been 10 people who were irritated that their doorbell was ringing early on a Saturday morning. Lots of no-answers. Lots of grumpy folks. Lots of no-sales. I remember in the summer months, if we were still on the street at 10:30 a.m. and had doughnuts left to sell, we were in trouble. The summer sun took its toll on the glaze and chocolate icing. It would have been nice to be able to call it quits and walk home. But my dad made sure that this was not an option. He dropped us off in neighborhoods that weren't within easy walking distance from home and told us he would pick us up at certain street corners at assigned times. We knew that if we showed up at those street corners with any doughnuts, we would be turned back on the streets again. Selling doughnuts at 2 o'clock in the afternoon in 90-degree heat was about as close to hell as I think I got when I was 8 years old.

My brother Wayne had the most difficulty with this arrangement. One morning, he simply couldn't take it. With three dozen left to sell and no hot prospects in sight, he simply dumped the doughnuts in a nearby street sewer. Today, Dale reports that he believes he may have been the inspiration behind this outrage. Though Dale was certainly capable of such an inspiration, the act itself smacks of Wayne. When my dad came to pick up Wayne, he simply feigned ignorance. He said he must have lost the money for those doughnuts through a hole in his pocket. It may have seemed lame, but with no doughnuts left, Wayne was permitted to go home to play with his friends. The ploy nearly worked. Unbelievably, when Sunday morning rolled around, my father decided to walk to church instead of taking the car. As luck would have it, we walked right past the street sewer where Wayne had disposed of the doughnuts. As luck would have it again, my dad saw the doughnuts. It wasn't a pretty scene. Any chance that Wayne had to figure prominently in my dad's business plans went out the window right there on that street corner. I don't think Wayne minded much.

Dale was also guilty of some doughnut shenanigans. Instead of dumping his doughnuts down the sewer, Dale sometimes decided that someone ought to enjoy them— even if he couldn't sell them. On occasion, he would pick out one of his newspaper route customers and simply leave one or two dozen doughnuts inside the storm door on the front porch. I wonder to this day if the people ate the doughnuts and what they must have thought about this unsolicited arrival of bakery products.

I think in any ordinary family, this ill-fated experiment selling doughnuts would have ended mercifully after a few weeks. But then, in any ordinary family, this ill-fated experiment would never have been attempted in the first place. My dad had bigger ideas. Upon discovering that there was a certain amount of "luck" in selling doughnuts door-to-door, he decided to put all the emphasis on preorders. No selling in the hot sun, no irritating sales pitches, no doorbells, only prepaid orders, the boys are done in a hurry and have their Saturdays free.

The plan was so good, he thought, that he would take it to others. By leaving printed circulars at people's homes in the neighborhood, he recruited boys throughout the city. During the week, the boys took orders for doughnuts. On Friday night, they phoned the orders in to our house. My dad phoned them on to the bakery. On Saturday morning, he would get the doughnuts and deliver them to the boys, who, in turn, delivered them to their customers. Instead of paper routes, my dad gave these boys the chance to have doughnut routes. Incredible as it may seem, the idea really took off. At the peak of the operation, there were about 25 boys around the city with doughnut routes—ordering 300 to 350 dozen doughnuts each week. But with this success came challenges. The Volkswagen Beetle has been touted for many things, but space isn't one of them. It was tough to fit all the doughnuts in one car load. We had to employ the services of our second car, a black 1956 Chevrolet. Between the two cars, we could pack in 350 dozen. I might mention here that after a morning workout transporting hundreds of dozens of doughnuts, our cars smelled like a doughnut shop. I know that even during the week, after a ride in either one of the cars, the family smelled like doughnuts. As it turned out, the smell of doughnuts was a smell that we would grow accustomed to. I wonder to this day if our social lives suffered.

I also remember some real fiascoes when the bakery couldn't meet the demand. Sometimes we had to scramble around to other bakeries in a wild attempt to pick up some of the shortage. When we couldn't come close to meeting the size of the order, customers had to be told that their doughnuts wouldn't be arriving until very late in the day. My dad became frustrated with things that went wrong when they were beyond his control. And this drove him to bigger and better things—or at least he thought so. After seeing the size of this operation and becoming convinced that doughnuts could be turned into money, my dad made the inevitable move to go into business full time.

Slip-Slidin' Away

Without noticing what was happening, my dad plunged onward and upward. There is a principle of new technology that some have written about that can be summarized by a lyric from Paul Simon's hit song *Slip-Slidin' Away*: "Ya know, the nearer your destination, the more you're slip-slidin' away." The idea behind the principle in new technology is that when human beings create solutions for certain problems, the solutions they create end up causing problems worse than the ones the solutions were intended to solve. I believe that something like this may have been operating in those early days when my dad developed the doughnut-route concept. The original scheme was designed to bring in more cash, free up his time for the family, and give him more personal autonomy. The doughnut-route concept did bring in more cash. But Friday nights were now devoted to taking phone orders. And Saturdays were taken up delivering doughnuts throughout the city. My dad was busier than ever. And his "free" time was being spent on the doughnuts—not on the family.

Recognizing these problems, my dad became convinced that the solution was to get bigger and get more control. In other words, get serious about doughnuts. In retrospect, the "slip-slidin' away" principle was at work again. The more control my dad gained over his own business, the less he was able to realize his initial goals. And that is precisely the theme of this chapter. My dad had to learn the hard way that the more he got what he wanted (a personal business), the less he *really* got what he wanted (more time with the family).

24 Hours a Day, 7 Days a Week

My dad didn't have the $50,000 that it took to get a doughnut franchise in the early 1960s. He had to seek a good portion of the money from at least one investor, who became a kind of private benefactor. Mr. Tutman is now dead, and I don't have any idea how much of his money was ever returned to him. My dad never really said. The impression I had was that Mr. Tutman didn't seem to mind that it was taking a while. He truly considered it an investment that he might never see again—not a loan. The $50,000 bought my dad the right to operate the doughnut shop under a popular and well-advertised name. It also bought him a formal contract—for 20 years—that came with a variety of stipulations. One of those stipulations was that the doughnut shop was a round-the-clock operation. With the exception of Thanksgiving and Christmas, the doughnuts had to be made. And there always had to be someone there to sell them. The most important implication of this contractual obligation was that the buck stopped with my family. If a baker didn't show up for work, my dad was the baker. If someone didn't show up to take care of the counter trade, my mom was generally the substitute. Fortunately for my parents, my brothers and I were also able to fill in on many occasions. Exactly how my parents failed to anticipate the demands of this situation, I will never quite understand. The toll that it took on the family was difficult to calculate.

Mark Redmund was about 70 years old and was part of the opening crew when our shop first opened its doors. My mom recalls what Redmund told her: "I guarantee you," said Redmund, "that if you still own this shop in five years, you will no longer be married to your husband."

Redmund spoke from experience. He had owned five doughnut shops in his lifetime and had a different wife to go with each one. Five shops and five wives. My parents beat those odds. Through their love for each other and what the family believes to be the grace of God, they survived the doughnut years with their marriage intact. When my dad passed away on October 24, 2007, my parents had just celebrated their 60th wedding anniversary the month before. My mom lived on for less than three years and joined him on April 7, 2010.

The first year in the franchise business, we rented a house about 5 miles away from the doughnut shop. Huge mistake. Home was too far away for my mom and dad to slip away from the business for the dinner hour. My brothers and I spent many nights fending for ourselves, heating TV dinners in the oven and fighting over who would get the Salisbury steak and who would get the chicken. My parents rectified the situation after a year and we moved into an apartment complex on the same block with the doughnut shop. This made it easier to get home quickly, but it also made it easy to run up to the shop for one thing or another. And there were plenty of reasons to run. I remember many a night when I was in junior high school that dinner came at 10:30 p.m. in a local diner—after my parents had finally managed to pull themselves away from the business after a grueling day of work. I think the thing that kept my parents pressing on was the hope that things would get better. And, over the 20-year period, there were some times that were relatively good. On a continuum, we were fairly well off. The business was basically good in terms of revenue and we had plenty of cash flow. My parents were able to send my brothers and me to college. We bought a boat (which, for many years, took up a parking space in the doughnut shop parking lot—against company policy, I'm sure). We even took a family vacation and got caught in the Woodstock traffic jam in upstate New York.

It was not that the doughnut shop did not provide a living; it certainly did. But it was not the kind of living my dad and mom had envisioned for the family. In many ways, the kind of living the doughnut shop provided was exactly the opposite of what my dad had wanted. He wanted more personal control over his time. Instead, he knew that at any given moment, he could be called to the doughnut shop for an emergency. He wanted more time with his kids. Instead, he often found it difficult to get *any* time with his kids. My brothers could each tell their own stories. For me, a few instances stand out.

It was a Saturday morning and I was in high school. That afternoon, my high school football team was going up against a formidable foe—the Rams. I remember the day well because the quarterback made our highly touted defense look silly. He just kept running around the ends for 15-yard gains. Eventually, this quarterback went on to an illustrious career in the NFL. My friend and I wanted desperately to go to the football game but we needed transportation. We made an arrangement for his father to take us to the game, and my father agreed to pick us up. I knew this meant that I would be depending on my dad. I was nervous. I knew he'd be working at the doughnut shop and I knew how 10 minutes could turn into 90 without even thinking about it. My mom was legally blind with a congenital retina problem that rendered her unable to drive. That afternoon, the 10 minutes turned into two hours. My dad just couldn't get away. There were doughnuts to be made. While I understood the demands of the business, I also felt the loss of not having my parents more in control of their daily schedule. In this case, there was the personal embarrassment of having a friend waiting on my dad. I still carry the image in my mind of standing on that street corner for two hours until after dusk set in. Finally, my father arrived.

The other image that is burned into my brain is the closing ritual on Christmas Eve. My dad and I would start to close the shop down around 4 p.m. Once the doors were locked at 5 p.m., I wanted us to be home celebrating the peace and tranquility of the holiday. But my dad always found something that needed to be done. Every 15 minutes, the phone would ring. It was my mom, telling me to hustle my father along. It couldn't be done easily. My dad could never turn a customer away. If someone failed to recognize that the store was closed and came up to the door, my dad would unlock the door to let the person in and then proceed to sell another cup of coffee or one of the few remaining doughnuts. Being the conversationalist that he was, my dad couldn't help himself. He was much more interested in chatting with another customer than he was in selling an extra cup of coffee or doughnut. I used to have an old photo that I took on one of those Christmas Eves when my dad was busy closing up shop and I had given up trying to pull him away. I will carry that image the rest of my days. It captured forever in my mind my dad's total dedication to making the business a success. The knowledge that I had of the rest of the family sitting home and waiting for his return is very much a part of that picture. It seemed that the harder my dad worked, the more elusive became the prize.

The Main Idea

The theme of this chapter is not that one should shy away from starting a business; rather, it is to alert those who aspire to their own business to open their eyes wide. **What seems like an alluring proposition for a great lifestyle and more time for the family might not turn out that way at all. Do good research. Know what you're getting into. Talk to others who know more than you do.** All of this sounds simple enough. But I am convinced that the image of money and leisure time, along with the fantasy of being your own boss, tend to blind the critical eye. Heed this word to the wise: Do your learning on the cheap—before you have to do it on the job. Our family did more than our share of learning on the job.

Chapter 3

Don't Plan on a "Family" Business Before You Ask the Family

The plan from the beginning was to have a "family" business. My parents had been inspired by a doughnut shop operation that they had observed months before they made the big move to get into the franchise business themselves. They were told that nearly every person who worked in that shop was a family member. My dad went to bed at night dreaming of his four boys each wearing a baker's cap and pleasantly going around the doughnut shop doing the various tasks that needed to be done. Together, we would watch the dough ($$) roll in. Of course, we'd have to grow up a little bit at first, but with three boys nearly in their teens when the doors of our business opened, my dad thought it would be no time at all until our family was the primary working unit that staffed the shop.

This was not a bad concept. But as we soon learned, one of the most difficult problems of the business was depending on other people who were not particularly trustworthy. Years later, when my dad reflected back on the doughnut years, I'm sure that a certain part of him still believed that if he could have somehow managed to turn the business into a true family enterprise, things would have worked out much differently. But it wasn't to be. I'm not sure that *anyone* could have taken four teenage boys and inspired them toward a career in a family doughnut business. What my dad sometimes saw as his great failure was probably an impossible dream. In a way, one of my parents' greatest struggles over the 20 years of operating the doughnut business—perhaps their greatest struggle—was trying to find a way for the family to be totally committed to the business. It just never quite worked out.

Dale Joined the Navy

I think my parents had already started to give up on the dream of the family business after just a few short years. When Dale graduated from high school, my parents seemed interested in having him take a shot at college, even though his high school grades were marginal. Dale did take a shot, but he missed the mark badly. He came home at Thanksgiving during his freshman year and never went back to that college. He had quite a lot of fun at school, but didn't pay much attention to studying. For a few months after his college misadventure, Dale worked at the doughnut shop and my parents discussed the possibility of his becoming a full-time manager. That idea must have been distasteful, because in March, Dale joined the Navy. He ended up serving in Vietnam for a year before returning and acquiring an early release from his term of duty. After that, he worked for the FBI in New York City and eventually left home again for another shot at college, this one proving more successful. With a degree in criminal justice, Dale made a career for many years with a state bureau of investigation. There was simply no way his life was going to revolve around a doughnut shop.

Wayne Discovered Cars and Girls

Wayne was the most difficult of the four of us in terms of cultivating a doughnut career. This was undoubtedly due in part to the fact that he had been confined to his room for years as a youngster with a rare and life-threatening kidney disease. When he was finally cured, it was like releasing a prisoner to freedom. Wayne had a lot of living to catch up on and he had the spirit to do it. Doughnuts just didn't figure into the mix.

Almost immediately after making the move to open up the doughnut shop, Wayne started showing delinquent tendencies. His interest in cars gradually led to several run-ins with the law. He was apprehended for being involved in the theft of a car battery and, as I mentioned earlier, he was frequently caught taking joy rides in my father's car before he had a license. The battery caper seemed innocent enough to Wayne. He and his friends were simply "borrowing" a battery from another car to see if their vehicle would start and run. After they had taken their ride, they fully intended to put the battery back in its rightful place. Unfortunately, the police intervened before they could complete the full cycle of battery changes. This was only the beginning of trouble where Wayne was concerned.

The doughnut shop was a virtual haven for teenage boys on the prowl. Not only were there all kinds of girls who came in as customers, there were also the girls who my parents hired—usually to serve as waitresses at the counter. It didn't take Wayne very long to get down to business.

There was an apartment complex just behind the doughnut shop, and Wayne met up with a young high school girl who lived in those apartments. It turned out to be convenient for him. Even when he was supposed to be doing something at the doughnut shop, he could slip down to those apartments to see his girlfriend. My parents didn't approve of the girl or Wayne's tendency to slip away when he was supposed to be working. Setting rules didn't help. For Wayne, rules were made to be broken. And break them he did. Eventually, he ended up marrying the girl, had a child with her, and went through a divorce. All of this took place after my parents had tried nearly everything to control his behavior. They sent him to military school for his last year of high school and shipped him off to Texas for a semester of college. It didn't work. Wayne had to pursue the girl. Today, Wayne looks back on all of this with some regret. He has been happily married for years to another girl he met in the same town. He just had to learn some of life's lessons the hard way. In any case, Wayne was a constant frustration to my parents' dream of establishing a family business. He just always seemed to be heading in a different direction.

Glenn Carried a Briefcase

In some ways, I must have seemed like the son with the most potential for the "family" business concept. I always saw the work as a chance to increase my bank account, even at age 12. But, alas, as I made my way through high school, my parents could see the writing on the wall. Unlike my brothers, I was oriented toward the life of a scholar. I actually liked school and I usually earned A's. My brothers tease me to this day that I was the only high school student on the planet who carried a briefcase. I don't know if they were right or not. I certainly *did* carry one. It seemed like the best way to organize my books and papers.

I was too shy to get into any serious trouble with girls and I didn't start to test the waters until my senior year in high school. By that time, my parents could see that I was college-bound. While they certainly encouraged me in this endeavor and were nothing but proud of my accomplishments, I always knew that there was a certain sadness at seeing me leave. Part of that sadness was that my loss was a huge blow to the family business concept. I worked in the shop more than any of my brothers did.

A major university was very close to the doughnut shop, and my parents had some hope that I would elect to stay close to home. I didn't. One of the factors in my decision was that I knew it would be far too easy for my parents to call the dorm room if they needed extra help in the doughnut kitchen. That kind of dilemma was one I wasn't interested in facing during my college years. I ended up leaving the area for a small liberal arts college in another part of the country. I never went back. It's hard to develop a family business when part of the family isn't there.

Garry Got Lost in the Shuffle

Garry was only 8 years old when we went into the doughnut business. The five years before he became old enough to help with the business in any significant way were fairly tumultuous ones. In retrospect, my parents often said that Garry got lost in the shuffle. Actually, Garry ended up working a fair amount in the shop through his high school years. But upon graduation, my parents felt obligated to offer him the option of going to college. It was either that or work full time at the doughnut shop. I think by the time Garry graduated from high school, the vision of a family business had all but faded away in my parents' minds. Garry decided on a degree at the local community college. He continued to work some hours in the doughnut shop, but it clearly wasn't his priority. After earning his two-year degree, my parents came back with the same offer: Work fulltime at the doughnut shop or enroll in a four-year institution and earn a bachelor's degree. Garry elected to earn the degree out of state, and when he graduated in 1979, he never again returned in any great working capacity to the doughnut shop.

Instead, he went into law enforcement work. My parents left the business five years later.

Leave the Sisters Alone

At some points my dad was so intent on the family business concept that he even entertained bringing his sister, who lived about 150 miles away, to serve as one of the workers. This idea was never implemented and it was probably good that it wasn't. First, there was reason to believe that my aunt would just not be able to handle the physical labor involved in serving customers or making doughnuts. Second, my aunt had a bit of a tendency toward the bizarre. We just couldn't trust her perceptions of reality. The following incident that I remember fondly should illustrate the point.

One weekend, my aunt had driven the 150 miles to see us. I don't remember exactly why she became angry with my dad, but for some reason, she decided that her visit had lasted long enough. Maybe my dad was trying to convince her to come live with us and work at the doughnut shop. She left the house at 12:30 on a Saturday afternoon. About an hour later, the doorbell rang and I was shocked to see my aunt standing in the doorway. I was even more shocked to hear what she had to say.

"OK, Glenn, someone is playing tricks on me." Not knowing how to respond to this curious statement, I simply asked, "What do you mean?" No one could have prepared me for what I was about to hear. My aunt proceeded to explain that she had driven her car to the highway and taken the entrance ramp that she thought would lead her home. Actually, she had gone north when she should have headed south. About 20 minutes later, she started to see signs with her name on them. Apparently, she didn't know that our state had a city with the same name as hers. I listened with wide eyes as my aunt accused someone in the family of putting those signs on the road to "trick" her. She said that she had no idea how we had managed to pull it off—but she was hopping mad about it. Still in disbelief, I tried to tell my aunt about the city that shared her name and assured her that the signs had been there for a long time. After explaining that she had gone north on the highway instead of south, I convinced her to try again. I could tell when she left the house that she still didn't believe a word I had said. I think she believed that I was the one behind the sign-conspiracy. Needless to say, my aunt would not have been a great prospect to build a family business around.

I often feel sympathy for my dad's dream of building a family business. When I look back and realize that our family was an unlikely bunch to form the core of the sort of operation my dad had envisioned, I feel a twinge of guilt—but only for a millisecond. There was no way that I was going to give my life to a doughnut shop. And I sure didn't expect my brothers to want to do it, either.

But What About the Boat?

My dad was a persistent man. He believed that one of the reasons his sons weren't buying into the vision of the family business was that we didn't properly understand that the business was going to be the source of good things in our life. To help us along, he proposed that Wayne and I enter into a partnership with him to buy a boat. We lived close to a river that one could use to ride all the way into the harbor of the metroplex. Initially, the idea of having our own speedboat was awesome. And we did take the boat out frequently in the summer months. Once, on the way to the city, we nearly sunk the boat in the middle of the bay. Given that the boat was half full of water, I don't understand how we managed to avoid a full sinking. But we did. In the end, though, the boat wasn't enough. For most of the year, it sat on the parking lot of the doughnut shop and took up a parking space. Eventually, we sold it. It would have taken more than a boat to motivate Wayne and me to commit all of our time to making doughnuts.

Hiring a Manager

The family business concept never truly died in my father's mind. If his own family couldn't do it, then maybe he could find someone new and try to make him into an extended family of sorts. About 10 years into the doughnut business, my parents hired a young man who we called "Tarzan" to manage the operation for them. This was done, in part, because my dad had decided to go back to work as an engineer to boost his salary. But the problem with hiring an outsider as a manager is that you never quite know who you have in the driver's seat. In our case, Tarzan turned out to be less than honest. My parents eventually determined that our manager was quite efficient at managing money that wasn't his so that it found its way out of our family's pockets and into his own bank account. I discuss this kind of predicament in more detail in the next chapter. It was a much bigger problem than we could have ever anticipated.

The Fish & Chips Experiment

One way that my parents tried to rein in Wayne's antics was by hiring him as the manager of a second business just a few blocks away from the doughnut shop. It almost worked. Wayne was married with a child and needed to find a steady job to support his family. I have saved the climactic story of the fish & chips experiment for a little later. The bottom line is that the business eventually failed. In retrospect, it would have probably made more sense to hire Wayne as the manager for the doughnut shop. But I think that my parents also wanted to venture out into a new project. After experiencing so many hard knocks in the doughnut shop, there was an appeal to making a fresh start and avoiding some of the same mistakes that had plagued the beginnings of the doughnut business. There was also the added incentive of trying to counteract a move made by the parent company of the doughnut shop. The company opened up another doughnut shop about two miles down the road from our store. That never quite made sense to me or to my parents. The negative impact that this could have had on sales was enough to scare my parents into believing that they needed another source of revenue. The fish & chips venture seemed like the sure ticket. But in the end, neither fish & chips nor doughnuts had the power to turn us into the kind of "business" family that my parents had envisioned.

Doughnuts and Church Didn't Mix

When the prospect of the immediate family devoting their lives to the doughnut business seemed to be on the wane, my parents decided that the next best option was to bring the church family into the enterprise. The pastor was already a regular each morning at the doughnut shop. He started his day with a cup of coffee and a doughnut. We always gave it to him for free. His daily presence in the shop helped trigger the idea that maybe what we needed was more church people in the store. My parents wondered whether we couldn't hire members of the church to cover our shifts. We tried. But the qualified and available members of our very small congregation were few and far between. The church family turned out to be a bigger bust than our immediate one. It just seemed like the whole idea of a "family" business of any kind wasn't to be.

Dale's wife, Nancy, remembers the time that she and Dale came to visit my parents after they were married. Nancy was a full-time nurse. While they were there, a counter worker called in sick. Incredibly, Nancy was called in for duty. And at the end of her shift, she discovered that the other counter worker had taken all of her tips and kept them for herself. It was only a few bucks, but Nancy was still stunned. At times, that's how it was at the doughnut shop. Experiences like these made you want to stay away because you knew if you went near it, you would be recruited for unpleasant duty.

The Main Idea

The idea of a family business is a great concept. But **it takes more than a great concept to make something work.** If the family consists of a group of adults who are absolutely committed to making the business a success, then maybe there's a chance. In our case, it proved to be too daunting a task to raise four boys so that they would go into the family business. In fact, even though they tried with me and each of my brothers, my parents couldn't manage to entice a single one of their sons to commit to the doughnut life.

Chapter 4

Learn the Techniques of a Thief So They Can't Be Used Against You

One of the major themes of the 20 years my family spent in the doughnut business was thievery. We were not prepared for this. We thought that thieves were really bad people who one was not likely to run into often. That proved to be the most naïve thought we ever had. In the doughnut shop, there was money. The lesson we learned was that wherever there was money, there was thievery. Sometimes it came from the outside and sometimes it came from the inside. My first direct experience with doughnut shop thievery was an encounter with the outside. It changed my life forever.

The Flimflam

I was 12 years old and had finally convinced my parents to let me serve a few customers at the counter. There was always talk about whether or not this violated child labor laws, but since we never saw any agents from the government armed with pad and pencil, we sort of ignored that. Plus, my parents told us that because we were the children of the business owners, the child labor laws didn't apply. I always suspected that they were wrong about that, but I didn't really care. I wanted to work.

I was supposed to work a one-hour shift to see how it felt. My mother trained me in customer relations and turned me loose. It was around 7 p.m., and it was raining lightly. For some reason that we never quite figured out, a light rain would increase business while a heavy rain would kill it. Predictably, the light rain brought in a flock of people and I was the only one there to serve them. One man bought two coffee rolls and paid the 70 cent sale with a $20 bill. I gave him some coins and 19 single bills and prepared to move on to another customer. But, before I could do so, the man asked me if he could have two $10 bills for the $20 in singles that he was now briskly counting out on the counter between us. He asked me to count it to make sure there was $20. He had pulled a $1 bill from his pocket and added it to the $19 in bills that I had just given him. I am not sure what in the world I was thinking (that was part of the flimflam art), but instead of taking the $20 to the register, depositing it, and getting the two tens, I went to the register first and retrieved the two tens and came back to the counter. The man was quick. He added the two $10 bills I had given him to the small pile of $20 that was sitting between us. He quickly picked it up and counted it out. Forty dollars. Then, he asked me to count it out to see if there was $40 in the pile. There was. Somehow, the fact that I was able to agree with him about this helped me ignore my feeling that something wasn't going right about this transaction. He asked me if he could have eight $5 bills for the pile of $40. Again, I went to the register to retrieve the money, leaving the pile on the counter. And once again, the man took the bills that I gave him with one hand and scooped up the pile of cash sitting between us with the other, counting furiously. He asked me for another transaction and we repeated the ritual. One more transaction later, and on my way down the counter to the second register to get more cash (because there were no bills left in the first register), I realized that something was very wrong. Why was the first register empty of any bills when all we were doing was exchanging money? When I turned around to challenge the man, he was gone. I immediately called my dad and told him I suspected that I had just been conned out of a large amount of money. When my dad arrived and cashed out the registers, we were $110 short. I had been flimflammed.

The police came down to the shop (yes, it's true—policemen love doughnut shops), and informed us that I was the fifth victim of a genuine flimflam artist who had been working the town that day. His MO was the same in every case: pick out a young worker, enter during a busy time when the worker was likely to be hurried, and count the money fast. The police informed us that he was a true pro and that I didn't have a chance. It didn't make me feel any better. I felt utterly stupid. And from that day onward, I was never quite the same. A guy had just come into the shop and stolen $110 from a 12-year-old kid. It hurt. In a very real way, it was the end of my age of innocence. I never quite looked at people the same way after that night. If you're going to go into business, beware of the many ways that people can steal from you.

An Easy Way to Steal Cigarettes

One of the stories that made its way around the circuit of doughnut shop owners had a very specific warning attached to it: watch your cigarette vending machines like a hawk. Apparently, a popular way to steal cigarettes was to case out a place like our doughnut shop and wait until the only worker in the store was a young high school girl who would typically work the counter during the relatively slow weekday shift, 3 p.m.-7 p.m. Two men would come in with a pickup truck and simply announce to the girl, "We're here to pick up the cigarette machine for repair." Before the naïve counter girl could blink, the cigarette machine was unplugged, loaded into the back of the pickup and hauled away to who knows where—never to be seen again. If it had just been fully loaded, the thieves got quite a take. This never happened in our store because my dad made sure that one of the first things he told new help was to never let anyone do anything to the property until he had been contacted first.

Phantom Flour

One of the most important times in the daily routine of a doughnut shop is when a semitruck pulls around back to the delivery door to bring in bags of flour, sugar, jelly, etc. The delivery person brings in the stock and then presents an invoice to be signed. My parents couldn't even begin to count the times they were cheated on their deliveries due to poor oversight at the precise time of the delivery truck arrival. Several things tended to happen. In the most common scenario, the delivery person would notice that no one was counting the order as it came in, or no one had asked for the invoice sheet to check off the delivery. In those instances, it was easy to keep a bag of flour or a can of jelly and get the employee to sign for the order. Whether that flour or jelly went back to the supply house to be sold again or whether it was sold for a cheaper price to another client didn't matter to my parents. We had paid for it and we didn't receive it.

Another way the delivery people would cheat would be to get the signature on the invoice *before* the products had actually been brought into the store. Once the signature is on paper, the truck can theoretically leave without delivering a thing. On more than one occasion, the truck only delivered a partial order after receiving a signature from my dad's employee, which said that everything had been delivered. There is no way to recover this loss since the delivery company has a signed invoice saying that everything listed was received.

It's hard to tell exactly how much money we lost this way over the years. One of the things that made deliveries difficult to control was the fact that orders came in at random times. Sometimes there was only one person in the store working the counter. This person could hardly do a diligent job counting the order while serving coffee and doughnuts to customers. My dad used to instruct the counter help to call him when an order arrived so that he could come check it in. But this didn't go over so well with the truck drivers, who were trying to make time. They often would not cooperate with the delay. I'm not sure we ever really worked out this problem in our 20 years in the business. I think we certainly were cheated more at the beginning until we learned the ins and outs of the daily operation. But I think we still lost money this way pretty regularly.

Whatever the case, if the thieves had just come from outside the business, we would have had comparatively few worries. The real threat of thievery came from the inside— from the employees themselves. When my parents went into their six-week training at the parent company, they were told that out of every three girls hired to work the counter, one would steal almost all the time, the second would steal some of the time, and the third would steal if she thought she could get away with it. While I think this was exaggerated to make the point, sometimes it seemed all too true.

Working from an Open Cash Drawer

If you've paid any attention at all to what happens when you make a purchase from a store, you've probably noticed that the retailer often has a sign posted that informs you that your purchase is free if you don't get a receipt. Perhaps you've wondered why the retailer would be so concerned that you, the customer, walked away with your receipt. The answer is simple: the retailer is trying to minimize thievery.

As it turns out, one of the most common ways for employees to steal money is to keep the cash register drawer open between sales. The employee will take the customer's money and deposit it into the register and give change so that the customer is oblivious to the fact that a crime is in progress. The employee then keeps track of how much money is going into the cash drawer, with no sales being tallied on the register. At an opportune moment, the employee stashes the built-up cash in a pocket or purse. The genius of this plan is that when the registers are cashed out and checked, there is no discrepancy between the sales tallied on the register and the cash in the drawer. It all matches.

There aren't many ways to deter this kind of theft. One way to do it is for the employer to use the customer in the battle. If the customer is expecting a receipt, then the sale has to be tallied up on the register. If the sale is tallied, the money has to be in the register or the theft will be detected. Thus, the retailer offers a small incentive to the customer to check the receipt. It's worth it. Another way we fought this technique of stealing was to show up randomly for register checks. If the data for a particular shift was showing unusually low sales, my parents would suspect that we were being robbed in this way. They would send me in whenever I was available during a suspect's shift to cash out the drawers. If we were "lucky" and I had gotten to the drawers before the employee could pocket the cash that was sitting there with no sales attached to it, our cash-check would show that the drawers had more money than we had sales. At first, it seemed a little strange to hear my parents complaining that we were $20 over on the cash-check. But, of course, they were complaining about the fact that the overage indicated that an employee had been planning the crime. The cash-check had thwarted it.

My parents instituted all sorts of rules to try to combat this kind of theft. They would not permit pockets on the uniforms of the counter workers. It didn't matter. Some of the girls would tuck the money inside their shoes. Then, at some opportune moment, they would grab their purse and make off to the restroom to empty their shoes out. My mother always said that if you came up with 100 ways to stop the theft, they would find method #101 to steal.

Watching Others Be Generous With Your Stuff

My parents were nice folks. They liked people and they tried to be kind to them. That showed up in the way they ran their business. One rule they had for their employees was that the consumption of food or drink behind the counter was forbidden. The rule made sense. Imagine coming in and picking out a dozen doughnuts while the waitress pauses in the middle to chomp through a jelly doughnut or slurp down some coffee. Not very appetizing. However, my parents permitted the employees to eat or drink whatever they wanted for free while they were on their 10-minute break. Over the years, we probably had a few people who were able to abuse that policy and gulp down a half-dozen doughnuts in 10 minutes. But that generally didn't happen. What did happen was worse.

Many of the employees tended to feel that if they didn't take advantage of our free-food policy while they were on their breaks, they had a subsequent right to pass out their free food to their friends. I remember one evening when the counter was lined up with about 10 teenagers who were all enjoying free doughnuts and beverages—courtesy of their friend who was working the counter for us. The strange part of this kind of theft was that many of the employees didn't even see it as stealing. They were just being generous. Unfortunately, they were being generous with the products that belonged to my parents. And my parents were trying to sell those products. There is no telling how many free doughnuts and beverages were distributed without our knowledge over the 20-year period. My guess is that if we had that money back today, we'd have quite a nice little bank account.

The Legacy of Lillian

The fact that the doughnut shop was a 24-hour-per-day operation made staffing a huge priority. As it turned out, the third shift (11 p.m. – 7 a.m.) was the toughest shift to cover with reliable help. I remember times when the family would sit around the living room and hold our collective breaths before we went to bed, waiting for an 11 p.m. phone call telling us that the night person had not shown up for work. If 11:05 p.m. came and went without a call, we knew we were home free with a good night's sleep—that is, until 5:30 a.m. rolled around and we had to worry whether one of our three bakers (who were all brothers hailing from Costa Rica) would show up to make the day's doughnuts. Having to work all night serving doughnuts and coffee after working a 12-hour shift earlier in the day was exhausting. But my parents did it plenty of times.

But then they got "lucky." A middle-aged woman who had prior experience working at a restaurant with a big-time reputation from a large metropolitan area applied to work the night shift. She was blunt and unattractive, she walked with a definite limp, and she almost always had her tongue hanging out the side of her mouth. Lillian was clearly capable of handling herself. She smoked more Camel cigarettes in an hour than I had seen anyone smoke in a lifetime. She was one tough lady. In a rare statement of her personal ethics, Lillian once told Dale, "Honey, I'd never lie to a kid, but I sure would lie to an adult." If my parents had only known before they hired her. As it was, Lillian seemed like just what my parents needed on the night shift. She was, literally, too good to be true. Night after night, seven days a week, Lillian reported promptly for work at 11 p.m. The town policemen knew her affectionately and she quickly developed a following of sorts. My parents would offer her a day off, but she always refused. "What else would I do?" she would reply. For years, my parents were able to relax when the night shift rolled around. Lillian was as dependable as the clock. She quickly became our highest-paid counter worker by a long shot. But years later, when we weren't expecting it, we had an incident that we found quite disturbing.

In a freak accident at home, Lillian broke her leg. She *had* to take some time off now. My parents quickly made plans to cover the shift with my brothers and me (it was summertime and school was out of session). Something remarkable happened. The first night my brother worked the shift and the registers were cashed out in the morning, my dad blinked twice when he saw that the night's sales were over $100 higher than the same night's sales a week before. That sort of increase was unusual. It could happen by chance, but it didn't seem likely. The next night was more of the same— another increase of $100 over the week before. It happened again on the third night...and the fourth...and the fifth.

Meanwhile, Lillian was calling daily and begging to come back to work on a walking cast. Given the strong correlation between Lillian's absence and higher store receipts, my parents insisted that she stay home. As the two to three weeks went by before Lillian could return to work, my dad computed an average increase in nightly sales of anywhere from $80 to $100. That works out to anywhere from $2,400 to $3,000 per month. Or $35,000 per year—unadjusted for inflation! Pretty amazing. If my parents had been able to save that amount of money every year that Lillian worked the night shift, they would have walked away from the business after 20 years with a nice retirement.

The next part of the Lillian story is, perhaps, the most incredible. You might think that once my parents learned that keeping Lillian on the night shift might mean giving up about $35,000 per year in addition to her salary, they would have never let her in the store again. But that's not what happened. They were faced with an impossible decision—either keep Lillian and rest in the knowledge that the third shift was covered, or do away with Lillian and wonder how to keep someone showing up for work each night at 11 p.m. My parents knew how hard it had been to cover that shift in the years before Lillian showed up. So they made their decision. Let Lillian continue in the job—and hope that the cash register receipts didn't drop back to their old levels. My dad did try to run some random cash-checks on Lillian's shift to try to figure out the pattern of the money—but I don't think he ever mastered the situation. I don't know what happened to Lillian after we left the business. I suspect that her retirement fund was more than adequate but I can't know that for sure. My parents' inability to find an alternative solution for the night shift speaks volumes about the daily strains of the business that could cause one to do things that, years later, look silly.

Becoming an Expert in Surveillance

My dad was not one to give up easily when faced with a problem. Throughout the 20 years of operating the doughnut shop, he tried to incorporate many different ways to deter theft. One of the first things he did was to cut out a rectangular space in the wall between the back storeroom and the customer counter. He installed a one-way mirror in that space, which permitted him to survey the counter workers while remaining undetected. He also tried to convince the counter workers that he had a complete television system in the store that he could view from home. Of course, he didn't. But some of the workers believed he did. Sometimes, after entering the store through a side door, he would take his place in the storeroom by the one-way mirror and have my mom phone the store at a pre-arranged time. My dad would wait until the counter worker answered the phone in the kitchen and then he immediately picked up the extension in the storeroom. Pretending that he had placed the call from home, my dad would then proceed to look through the one-way glass and ask the counter worker various questions about things that were taking place in the store at that moment. This really caused the workers to think twice about the exact security system that my dad had installed. It probably worked to deter some theft.

After talking with an electronic surveillance company, my dad also purchased two devices that he thought would help. The first was a door counter that registered the number of times the main door at the entrance of the store was opened. By monitoring this counter and correlating it to sales, he obtained some data that helped him find out if the amount of money in the registers was appropriate given the number of customers who had entered the store. The second device was like nothing I knew even existed. It was a simple whistle that had somehow been tuned to a frequency that our store telephone would recognize. My dad could dial the store's number and blow the whistle into the telephone at the same time. The whistle caused the phone at the store not to ring, but to activate the phone such that my dad could hear everything that was going on in the store. It was a neat trick. But, unfortunately, the employees didn't often talk about their theft while they were doing it. This kind of audio monitoring didn't prove very effective at actually catching a thief.

Despite all of the best electronic devices, theft was difficult to stop. Once, during a period when coffee prices were skyrocketing, my dad went outside to the dumpster to find an empty box that he wanted to use for a container. He spotted a good one sitting right on top the dumpster. When he reached for it, he noticed that it was heavy. Upon examination, he found that it was an unopened case of 30 pounds of coffee. It didn't take much thinking to realize that someone had set the box there so it could be easily picked up. The back of the store where the dumpster was located was an ideal spot for picking up goods without anyone noticing. This old trick is still prevalent in businesses around the country. In fact, when I told this story to a good friend, he immediately recalled a time not too long ago when he was hunting for good storage boxes at the rear of a local beer and wine shop. To his dismay (and joy), he discovered a full carton of beer amid the empty boxes. He instantly realized that he had intercepted an intended pickup.

In the end, catching a thief wasn't something we wanted to do, anyway. One morning, my dad went back to the storeroom to get some flour and he noticed a small brown bag sitting by the edge of one of the storage shelves. It appeared to be a bag lunch, but just to make sure, he opened it up and peered inside. What he saw was most interesting. Instead of a sandwich, he saw a brand new box of tea bags—the same kind that we stocked and used to serve tea to our customers. My dad reasoned that someone was planning to take those tea bags home. Instead of foiling the plan, my dad carefully opened the tea bag box and placed a small note on top before closing the box and restoring it to the lunch bag. The note was my dad's paraphrase of a verse from the Bible: "Be ye sure your sins will find you out" (Numbers 32:23). At the end of the morning counter shift, my dad noticed that the lunch bag had disappeared from the storeroom. The next morning, our best morning-shift counter worker called in and said that she would be unable to work there anymore. My dad caught the thief, but he lost a reliable counter worker at the same time.

The Main Idea

If you're going into business, **be prepared for people to try to steal from you. Learn their techniques *before* you get into business by talking to others who own businesses similar to the one you're thinking about. Never underestimate the capacity for other people to take things that belong to you; don't be fooled into thinking that "nice" people don't steal**. My parents never met a crook they didn't like. Finally, think carefully about the fact that your view of people will undoubtedly change as a result of dealing with the sorts of people that I've described in this chapter. After a while, virtually everyone became a potential suspect. This was an insidious mentality that profoundly affected the dynamic in our family. Perhaps it is no accident that my three brothers all ended up in careers associated with criminal justice. With all those crooks out there, something had to be done.

Chapter 5

Be Careful Who You Hire—It Matters

In some small businesses, it may be possible to get along without hiring anybody. If you can manage to keep only one person's hands on the money—your own—then you've put yourself at a tremendous advantage. But in the doughnut business, this was simply not possible. Many people had to be hired: bakers, counter workers, porters (janitors), doughnut finishers, window washers, etc. In this chapter, I'll recount some of the more colorful characters who worked for my parents. The purpose of these narratives is to make the point clear that no amount of research done on a prospective employee is wasted. In the doughnut business, my parents often perceived the need for help to be so great that any warm body was acceptable. That mindset contributed to some interesting encounters with some rather strange people over the years.

During 20 years of hiring doughnut-shop workers, there is no question that my parents had their share of poor hires. Of course, our screening procedure was not very elaborate. I remember working the counter at various times when someone came in off the street and wanted to apply for a job. My instructions from my parents were to give the person a paper bag that we used for take-out coffee and have him or her flip it over to the side that had no advertising. The applicant was instructed to leave his or her name, phone number, address, hours available, and prior experience. Hiring a new person was often a matter of "going through the bags" until we found someone who was still interested in a job. Below, I catalog some of the results of this elaborate screening process.

Tina—Fading into the Fog

I have already mentioned the fact that the most difficult shift to fill with reliable help was the 11 p.m. - 7 a.m. One of the most unusual people that we ever hired to fill this shift was Tina. Actually, Tina had been a fairly reliable employee for about two to three weeks and my parents were encouraged about Tina's long-term prospects. But that optimism came crashing down with a single phone call at 3:30 in the morning. While we were accustomed to getting phone calls at all hours, not many calls came in the dead of night. And not many of them came from police officers.

"Mr. Sparks?" the officer said in a strange tone. "You've got a problem up here at the doughnut shop. I came in the store about 25 minutes ago and there was no one here to serve me. And there's still no one here. In fact, Mr. Sparks, I don't know how long your store has been empty. But I think you'd better get someone up here."

"Isn't Tina there?" my father asked indignantly, knowing thatall of the police officers knew our night help by name.

"No, sir, she's not," answered the officer. At that moment, a customer walked into the store and the officer recognized him as a regular night customer, so he asked if he had seen Tina.

The customer replied, "Sure have. Tina met a guy at about midnight, and at about a quarter to three she just folded up her apron and they walked out hand-in-hand. When I last saw them, they were walking over the bridge. They disappeared into the fog at about ten to three."

And that was the last we ever saw of Tina, at least as an employee. Tina never came back to claim her paycheck. She never called to explain her behavior. She just walked off in the middle of the night, leaving our cash registers full of money for anyone to take. Incredibly, though some of the customers seemed to know what had transpired, no cash was missing. More than a year later, Tina came back into the doughnut shop as a customer. She had an infant in a stroller (perhaps conceived during the time when she should have been working the counter) and she greeted my parents with a smile, never mentioning the night that she had walked off her shift. It was as if that had taken place in a different lifetime and she was no longer accountable for it.

Tarzan

Tina wasn't the only mysterious deserter we had to cope with. Tarzan was a nickname for a young man that my dad hired as both a baker and a finisher. He learned to do both very well. But one day, in the middle of his shift as a doughnut finisher, he simply walked out of the store with no explanation. We found out later that he had gone to work for another store that was owned and operated by the parent company. In fact, he worked at the company store for several years. Then, just as suddenly as he had walked away, he phoned my dad one day and, incredibly, asked for his job back. Even more incredibly, my dad hired him back. Tarzan was a good talker and my dad was a fairly soft touch. Not to mention the fact that at the time Tarzan called, my parents desperately needed someone to make doughnuts. We eventually hired Tarzan as a store manager.

Doughnut Bakers from Costa Rica

The first time I told my wife, Cheri, about the three bakers who worked for my dad during most of the doughnut years, she nearly rolled on the floor with laughter. She simply couldn't believe that we had a trio of brothers from Costa Rica with these names: Felipe Diaz Alou (known as Old Felipe because he was the oldest brother); Felipe Alou Diaz (known simply as Felipe); and finally, Eddy. I don't even remember which last name Eddy used. I would say that 75 percent of the doughnuts made over the 20-year period were made by one of the Alou brothers. Needless to say, they were very important to the life of the business. Old Felipe was a man of few words and always seemed to have a short fuse. He rarely smiled and seemed to carry the weight of the world on his shoulders. His younger brother, Felipe, was also a man of few words, but he had a mellow disposition. He would talk to me frequently about boxing matches and horse races. He seemed content with his life, especially if he was winning his bets. Eddy had obviously spent more time in the U.S. than the other two had. He was rather extroverted and spoke better English than did his brothers.

The fact that the middle and last names were reversed for the two brothers named Felipe was a great curiosity to us. We thought that maybe this was how it was done in Costa Rica. Maybe there was some method to this system of naming that we never learned. But one thing we knew for sure was that the two Felipes used their names to totally confuse the authorities.

One day, a person from the immigration department stopped by the doughnut shop looking for Felipe Alou. As I sprinkled powdered sugar on the doughnuts, I listened to the conversation with interest. I certainly thought that the immigration man had found Felipe Alou. But, feigning very poor English, Felipe explained to the man that he was Felipe *Diaz*, not Felipe Alou. I heard Felipe say, "My brother—he Felipe Alou." The immigration man furrowed his brow and asked where his brother could be found. "He work tomorrow," came the answer. The next day, when the immigration man paid another visit, I'll never forget the look on his face upon hearing the words, "Me, Eddy." "My brother who work yesterday—*he* Felipe Alou." There followed a 10-minute conversation where the two phrases that I heard over and over were "Diaz-Alou" and "Alou-Diaz." The immigration man looked so confused after all of this that I think he gave up. Eddy gave him a free cup of coffee and bid him farewell. We never saw the man again. That was just fine with my dad. He became nervous when people like that showed up to talk to his bakers. The bakers needed to be protected at all costs.

The Alou brothers lived across the river from our store. I remember many mornings making the drive with my dad across the river at 5:30 a.m. to knock on their door (they all lived in the same apartment) to wake one of them up. No baker had shown up at 5:00 a.m. and, rather than be tied down to baking for the day, my dad preferred to take the time and see if we could rouse one of the Alou brothers. If Felipe couldn't come in (usually due to a hangover), then there was a chance that old Felipe could come in. If we struck out on both Felipes, then Eddy was a possibility. Amazingly, about half of these trips were successful. The other half saw my dad and me driving to the shop together to gear up for a day of doughnut making. When all of the Alou brothers were out of commission, the day was going to be a bad one, guaranteed. For one thing, my dad was a perfectionist when he baked the doughnuts. That was fine, except it meant I would have to work a 10-hour day as the doughnut finisher instead of a 6-hour day. It literally took my dad almost twice as long to produce the same quantity of doughnuts that one of the Alou brothers could produce. My dad always claimed that he could go just as fast as the Alous. But he never did.

For people who don't know the doughnut business, the fact that my parents had to rely on three brothers who sometimes couldn't make it to work after a night of drinking may seem strange. Why not hire someone else? It sounds easy, but it wasn't that simple. The job of a doughnut baker is what I refer to as a "semi-skilled" job. It took at least two months (and maybe three) to teach someone how to perform all the tasks involved in doughnut baking. There was a considerable amount of hand and finger dexterity required. The basics could be taught in a day or two, but it took weeks before the baker was really able to do the job well. Although there was a fair amount of skill involved, it was not a high-paying job. Usually, people who had the skill to learn the position were able to get better jobs. Consequently, good doughnut bakers were difficult to find and it was hard to train new ones. Thus, when my father had the good fortune to find three brothers who could all do the job, he continued to work with them for as long as he could, even though they frequently needed to be nurtured and coddled.

Christmas was a particularly difficult time for baking the doughnuts. That was because Felipe, Felipe, and Eddy always informed my parents that they had to return to Costa Rica because their father (Old Old Felipe) was very sick. We never knew exactly when the brothers would return. Usually, it was well into January. One year, my dad managed to phone them in Costa Rica and they explained that their father had died and hat they would be back after the funeral. But, the following Christmas, my parents realized that there was no truth to the story about Old Old Felipe's death. Once again, my parents were informed that the brothers-three would be traveling to Costa Rica to visit their father, who was gravely ill.

"I thought your father died last year," said my father to Felipe.

"No, he *almost* die. But he get better," answered Felipe.

After a few years, my parents simply became used to the fact that at Christmas time, Old Old Felipe always got sick. He nearly died every January and then recovered so that the brothers could come back to the States. As far as we know, Old Old Felipe may still be alive today. In any event, he suffered the most predictable illnesses of anyone on the planet. I will never forget the sheepish grin on Felipe's face when he told my father each year that he was going to Costa Rica because his father was sick. I don't know how many times this annual ritual was played out over the years, but it seemed to become part of the holiday itself. We knew another year had passed when Old Old Felipe got sick for Christmas.

Doughnut baking was such a necessity in the business that one of the company men once told my dad that if your baker came to work one day and said that he had just murdered his wife, the most likely response from the shop owner would be, "Here, wipe the blood on my apron and get to work." This oft-repeated comment in the years of our doughnut making turned out to be a little too close for comfort. During a crisis time when none of the Alou brothers were around to work, my father hired a baker who he later discovered was wanted for murder. As I recall, in the later years, there was even suspicion that our beloved Eddy was mixed up in a murder in the local community.

Jack—the Baker with the Ax

While we may have wondered about Eddy's involvement in a murder, with Jack there was no doubt. A local FBI agent introduced Jack to my father on the chance that my father would hire him. Jack had just finished a 20-year jail term for murdering his mother-in-law by taking an ax to her skull. I never felt totally comfortable working in the kitchen with Jack after I learned about his history. But he turned out to be a good doughnut baker. He had learned the craft while he was in prison.

Jack—the Boy with a Screwdriver

The family will never forget Jack Blickman. My father hired him to mop the floors. I never quite figured out what made Jack tick. He seemed incredibly stupid in terms of what he knew about the world around him, and his social/emotional intelligence quotient must have been near the bottom of the scale. But he seemed to have some measure of technical aptitude. Unfortunately for us, Jack often exercised this aptitude on the premises of our doughnut shop when he was supposed to be mopping floors. We should have known that we were in trouble with Jack when, shortly after he was hired, he announced to anyone who would listen that he was "getting the blahs from mopping the flaahs." One evening, my father walked into the kitchen to inspect the job that Jack was doing and his face fell. There on the kitchen floor was every small screw, nut, washer, electric switch, etc. from the large electric mixer that was used daily to mix the large quantities of dough for the doughnuts. My father's face wrinkled in that look of utter disgust he sometimes had. The conversation that followed reminded me of a conversation between Gomer Pyle and Sergeant Carter. My dad bellowed, "What the Sam Hill is going on here?" Jack may not have known it yet, but when my father used the name of "Sam Hill," someone was in trouble. This time it was Jack. Jack's reply was matter-of-fact—much too calm for a question that had invoked the name of Sam Hill: "Well, I just got to looking at this mixer and I wondered what really made it work. The only way you can really answer that question is to take it apart. Don't worry, Mr. Sparks, I'll put it back together again." My dad's face grew red, and the two of them began to reassemble the mixer. As I recall, a service repairman had to be called out on an emergency visit to replace some parts that Jack couldn't quite put back correctly. The mixer was not the only appliance that Jack took apart. My parents claimed that by the time he left our employment, he had disassembled nearly every mechanism in the store and attempted to put it back together again. Sometimes, he succeeded in getting the appliance back together. Most of the time, he failed.

On one occasion, Jack managed to tinker long enough with the fire protection system that he set it off. Instantly, the entire kitchen was covered with a spray of white foam. Every piece of equipment, including the baking tables, the doughnut screens, the vats of shortening, etc. was completely contaminated. It took hours and hours to clean it up, not to mention the $400 it cost to recharge the entire fire-protection system.

On another occasion when Jack was assigned to clean the doughnut fryers, he filled them with water after emptying out the shortening and brought the water to a boil. The only thing he did wrong was to leave the water boiling until it all boiled away. The intense heat burned a hole in the fryers. When my dad called the fryer manufacturer, they were amazed at the fact that the fryer had burned out. They told him that the fryers could last for 100 years and they almost never had customers file a claim on the 10-year warranty. Fortunately, the warranty did cover the replacement because the fryers were not quite 10 years old when the incident took place, and the warranty extended to accidents such as the one that Jack's behavior precipitated. Sometimes, we got lucky.

The obvious question here is why did my parents continue to offer Jack employment? The answer has to do with my dad's eternal optimism and commitment to helping people who he thought could be helped. It wasn't always good business. But my dad couldn't help it. Actually, my dad released Jack once or twice, only to rehire him. During one of the periods when Jack wasn't working for us, he worked for a local delicatessen. The woman who owned the deli talked occasionally with my parents and, one day, told them an incredible tale. When she had turned to her meat slicer to make a sandwich for a customer, she discovered that the slicer was sitting on the counter in dozens of pieces. Jack had struck again.

After that, I heard that Jack was a technician in the armed forces. He was responsible for servicing jet fighter planes. I have sometimes thought that this might go a long way toward explaining all of those missing planes that supposedly fly into the Bermuda Triangle and never return. Maybe those planes were serviced by Jack Blickman.

More recently, before my mother passed away, she told me an unbelievable story about Jack that I have no reason to doubt. Upon leaving the military, Jack was hired by the local hospital and put in charge of the physical plant, with special oversight over the hospital's electrical system. All went well until one afternoon when the hospital lost power. In fact, the backup power system had also failed. Imagine the poor patients who were having delicate surgeries when the power went out. In the madness that followed, hospital supervisors searched for Jack. They found him. He was poised in front of the main electrical circuit boards of the hospital—with parts all over the floor. He was trying to discover "how things worked." I understand that it took several hours for the hospital to restore things to normal. I suppose that Jack hadn't learned very much since the days when he took the doughnut mixer apart. The hospital dismissed him promptly. I never heard any of the gory details from the medical procedures that were interrupted by the power failure. It's probably just as well.

Vicky—Arrested for Her Appearance

One of the oddest employees my parents ever hired was Vicky. She didn't last very long. She was hired for an early morning shift and she took the bus to work. The bus let her off about two blocks from our store. One morning, Vicky got off the bus and proceeded to start the short walk to our store. But for some reason, she was clothed in a bathrobe and sleeping cap—like the one worn by the father in my childhood story book version of *The Night Before Christmas*. The cops in our town were definitely small-town cops, Barney Fife types. They could sniff out a problem when there wasn't a problem for miles around. In this case, I'll never know if there was a problem or not. Vicky's choice of attire really was strange. The cops thought it was *too* strange. They picked her up before she arrived at work. Someone from the family had to cover Vicky's shift. I don't think Vicky ever returned to work for us.

Rachel—the Doughnut Twirler

Whenever a new employee was trained to work the counter, my mother was usually the one who served as trainer. She took several hours to explain the nuances of waiting on a customer politely and properly. When a doughnut was ordered with coffee, the waitress was to take a piece of special paper from a dispenser and take the doughnut out of the tray while wrapping the paper around it in order to avoid any direct contact with the fingers or hands. The customer was served with the doughnut resting on the paper so that it wouldn't make direct contact with the countertop.

After going through the full training ritual with Rachel, the time came for her to serve her first customer. A distinguished-looking gentleman requested a cup of coffee and two glazed doughnuts. After Rachel served the coffee carefully, she walked down to the doughnut cases and proceeded confidently. She passed the dispenser containing the paper that she was supposed to use. Instead, she walked over to the doughnut tray and stuck one of her index fingers into the hole of one doughnut and the other index finger into the hole of another. She turned around and proceeded back to the customer, twirling the two doughnuts on her respective index fingers. When she arrived at the customer's stool, she continued to twirl the doughnuts until they spun off her fingers and onto the counter next to the coffee cup. My mother was frozen in silent horror. There hadn't been any advance warning that her trainee was mentally challenged. Needless to say, Rachel didn't last very long as a waitress.

Billy—Following in My Brother's Footsteps

I don't know what it is about doughnuts. As I reported earlier, my brother Wayne had dumped some down the sewer when he couldn't sell them on his doughnut route. A young teenager named Billy who my parents hired to finish the doughnuts decided that the "throw-away" strategy wasn't a bad idea. As far as I know, he had never even talked with my brother. He just came up with it all by himself. In this case there were more than a few dozen doughnuts at stake. Each flat screen of doughnuts held about three dozen. The screens were stored on racks that could hold as many as 20 screens. One afternoon, Billy decided that the one rack of doughnuts he had finished was enough. There was only one problem—he was supposed to finish two racks. This was a very tough problem for Billy. Somehow, he had to get rid of that second rack of unfinished doughnuts. In an act that was even more stupid than my brother's when he threw the doughnuts into the sewer, Billy took the doughnuts on that second rack and threw them out the back door into an alley. My dad, having had past experience with finding good doughnuts that had been thrown away, discovered the crime. Billy had thrown away his last doughnut—at least in our store.

Nancy—My Future Sister-in-Law

I suppose it was inevitable that with four boys (my three brothers and me) and all of the high school counter girls working part time and weekends, chemistry would take its natural course. When Nancy was hired, there was nothing about her that could have clued me in to the fact that my brother Dale was going to fall hard. But that's exactly what happened. On Saturday mornings, the counter trade was often handled by Dale and Nancy. To anyone who bothered to watch, there was obviously a rich tapestry of flirtatious games taking place between the two of them as they provided coffee and doughnuts for the customers. I was just young enough to find the whole thing sickening. Eventually, Dale and Nancy got married and they remain so today. As it turned out, it really did matter who my parents hired. In the case of Nancy, they ended up with a family member and mother of their grandchildren. This was one case where a hire worked out far better than we expected.

The Main Idea

The point of introducing Tina, Tarzan, Felipe, Felipe, Eddy, Jack, Jack Blickman, Vicky, Rachel, and Billy is to underscore the idea that **sometimes, even after your best research, your employees might not be ideal in every respect.** No matter how well-intentioned you are when you begin your business operation, you might find that the structure of the business leaves you with some less than desirable folks that you have to depend on. Good communication skills and a willingness to work with people of all types serve the business well. Sometimes, there is simply no other way. Nevertheless, it would have probably paid off in the end for my parents if they had actually done thorough reference checks, administered a few aptitude tests, and conducted more extensive interviews as an alternative to "going through the bags." In the case of Nancy, we just lucked out.

Chapter 6

Attorneys, Accountants & Insurance Agents: Handle With Care

If you're contemplating going into business, there is probably nothing you can do to avoid it—you will have to hire an attorney (probably more than one) somewhere along the line, probably sooner rather than later. And unless you're a tax expert in your spare time, you'll also need an accountant. In a business like ours, liability insurance and worker's compensation were musts. They had to be purchased through an insurance agent. Once again, as in so many areas of small business, it pays to do some research before you hire these professionals to work on your behalf. In the case of my parents, I think they hired well. Nevertheless, they learned along the way that *thinking* that you've hired well does not protect you from certain surprises. In our case, the surprises were almost always bad. The stress that these surprises added to the daily operation of the business was incalculable.

You Think You've Paid Your Payroll Taxes? Think Again.

My dad will never forget the day that a young man walked through the door of the doughnut shop and identified himself as an agent of the Internal Revenue Service. My dad was not accustomed to dealing directly with the IRS. The payroll taxes were routinely handled by Mr. Roperstein, a prominent accountant in the city who had come highly recommended to my parents from local business operators. I remember one afternoon when my parents drove by Mr. Roperstein's house. It appeared to my young eyes to be a huge brick mansion perched on top of a hill. Clearly, Mr. Roperstein was doing well. My parents had trusted their payroll to a real expert. They joked as we drove by the mansion that it made them feel somewhat proud to say that the man who lived in that house worked for them. But, as my dad was about to find out from the IRS, he may not have understood the exact nature of the work that Mr. Roperstein was doing.

As my dad fell silent, the IRS agent explained that the records showed that my parents had failed to pay their payroll taxes for a long time. They owed over $15,000 and the agent was there to collect it. If he couldn't get the taxes, the store would have to be closed down. My dad was incredulous. Mr. Roperstein had been paid regularly to handle our payroll and all the taxes due to the IRS. My parents had dutifully given the payroll taxes to Mr. Roperstein and had trusted that they had always been paid on time. Somewhat flustered and not knowing exactly what to say, my dad said something about the fact that he always paid his taxes to Mr. Roperstein. He then asked the IRS agent to please wait at the store while he checked in at home, just two doors down, to find out what was going on. He instructed the counter worker to serve the IRS agent anything he wanted without charge (my dad knew when courtesy was mandated) and quickly exited.

Once he got home, he placed a phone call to Mr. Roperstein. When Mr. Roperstein heard what had happened, he dropped everything and raced over to the apartment complex where my parents lived. "Meet me downstairs on the parking lot," commanded Mr. Roperstein. In the meeting that followed on the parking lot, my dad received a bit of insight into the fact that things were not always as they seemed.

The first thing my dad noticed was that Mr. Roperstein was visibly nervous. He paced frantically around the parking lot of the apartment house as he contemplated what to do. He was also angry. "Listen," he told my dad. "Never tell *anyone* about who you pay your tax money to. If anyone asks about your taxes, just say that you'll have to contact your accountant." Mr. Roperstein was clearly upset about the fact that my dad had actually identified him by name to the IRS agent as the one who received his money. Of course, my dad clearly started to suspect that perhaps Mr. Roperstein was using his tax money for something other than paying the taxes. The look on my dad's face must have communicated his astonishment at even considering the possibility. "Look," said Mr. Roperstein. "You don't understand that I sometimes do business in unusual ways." Who knew the nature of these unusual ways? My dad certainly didn't. Perhaps Mr. Roperstein was using the money to invest in short-term stocks, hoping that the payoff would be enough to pay the IRS when it came calling, while still having some cash left over to fund the lifestyle at the big brick mansion. Mr. Roperstein never told my dad why the money had not been paid on time. And Mr. Roperstein's emotional state was enough to scare my dad away from asking too hard. In the end, Mr. Roperstein assured my dad that he would take care of things. They went upstairs to the apartment and called the IRS agent, who was still sitting at the doughnut counter enjoying a cup of coffee. Following a brief phone conversation, Mr. Roperstein went to the doughnut shop to meet the agent. That was the last my parents heard from the IRS about their payroll taxes. It was also all they ever heard from Mr. Roperstein about where their money had gone. They decided not to ask. I suppose all's well that ends well. Perhaps there had been no impropriety going on at all. We never discovered what the incident was really about.

When You Hire a Lawyer, Get Ready to Pay... and Pay... and Pay...

My dad's experience with Mr. Roperstein was a little different from his experience with Mr. Marreroman, his personal attorney. But it still revolved around money. I was never really sure how good an attorney Mr. Marreroman was or how many other clients he had. Given the time that he spent on the phone with my parents, I wondered how he could have any time left over for anyone else. Mr. Marreroman always seemed a bit strange to me. After a long marriage, he divorced his wife when they were both well into their sixties. In a conversation with my mother he attempted to explain his action. During preparations that they were making for a trip, Mr. Marreroman discovered that the birth date on his wife's passport meant that she was actually five years older than he had thought. In a voice of astonishment, Mr. Marreroman said, "Mrs. Sparks, can you imagine what it was like for me? I woke up one morning and looked at my wife and realized that she was not the same woman I had married. She looked *old*. No wonder we've been incompatible all these years." Perhaps my parents should have realized that it might not be a good idea to hire an attorney who found getting old to be grounds for divorce. I don't really know how my parents managed to find Mr. Marreroman in the first place. They were told that he had a degree from the Ivy League and had graduated with honors. But I think all they really knew is that he lived close by and sometimes came in for coffee. These are not good hiring criteria. On the other hand, if you don't have time to do research, they are certainly easy criteria to use.

After a long and complex negotiation that Mr. Marreroman had handled for a dispute that my parents had with the parent company of the franchise, he sent my parents a bill for $1,350. My mom called Mr. Marreroman to explain that we simply couldn't pay this amount as a lump sum and requested a payment plan. After deciding on a down payment, my mom agreed to send a check for $100 on the first of each month until the bill was paid. Heaven forbid the check was ever a day late. At 9 a.m. the day after it was due, the phone would ring and Mr. Marreroman would remind my parents that he had not yet received his check. Often, it was already in the mail.

Finally, my parents were within $150 of paying off the bill and my mom decided to write a final check for the entire balance. She enclosed a note that informed Mr. Marreroman that after this check was paid, there would be no more payments. Mr. Marreroman promptly cashed the $150 check. When the next month's usual payment date came and went, my parents' phone rang at 9 the next morning. "Mrs. Sparks," roared Mr. Marreroman, "I didn't get my check yesterday."

"I know, Mr. Marreroman," my mom replied calmly. "Didn't you read the note I sent you last month stating that the balance was now completely paid?"

There was a long silence. Finally, Mr. Marreroman spoke: "Well, Mrs. Sparks, I guess I'll have to recapitulate my figures." My parents received another large bill a few days later. They ignored it. This proved to be the end of their relationship with Mr. Marreroman. At least he didn't try to sue for the recapitulated amount.

Don't Fall Off a Ladder Unless You're Insured

If dealing with personal accountants and attorneys were not enough, my parents discovered that not even insurance agents could be trusted. It was common practice in the doughnut business to get to know other managers of the stores in the general area. My parents knew several other store operators and it was natural to exchange information with these people who were in a similar situation. Early on in our adventure in the doughnut business, through one of these conversations, my parents received a tip on a "good" contact for liability insurance. Insurance was something that you couldn't afford to be without.

The doughnut shop could actually be a dangerous place. There were 100-pound bags of sugar and flour that could cause back injuries upon lifting. There was a huge mixing machine for the dough that everyone soon learned to respect. Several stories circulated around the doughnut shops that told of bakers who had gotten their aprons caught in the mixer and had literally been dragged into the huge bowl of flour as the mixing paddle revolved at high speed. This was the kind of "rolling in dough" that one desperately wanted to avoid. Of course, the kitchen floor was always wet and constituted a real hazard to an unsuspecting individual. And the huge vats of hot shortening that were used to fry the doughnuts were the ultimate threat. Like the mixer stories, many horrendous tales circulated about bakers who had either fallen or been pushed into the fryer. One of the bakers used to tell me that if I placed my finger in the hot fryer for 10 seconds, it would burn down to the bone. That was enough to give me serious concern for my own well-being whenever I was anywhere near the doughnut fryers. Sometimes I had to step in for an emergency and do the frying. I can't remember ever frying a screen of doughnuts without getting at least a little hot grease splashed on my hands.

Given the many risks of injury around the doughnut shop, it would have been unthinkable to scrimp when it came to insurance. When my parents heard from their fellow operators that there was a good general insurance agent who could take care of their liability needs, they made the phone call. Mr. Edwards was nice, efficient, and seemingly credible. My parents wanted to be worry-free in this area, so they quickly bought the policy that Mr. Edwards recommended and that the other stores had all purchased. They were covered. No sweat. No worries.

One day the phone rang. It was the operator of the store that was located about 20 miles away. My parents knew him well. "Mr. Sparks," he started. "I'm afraid you're not going to believe what I'm about to tell you." "Go ahead, try me," replied my dad. By this time in the business, he was getting used to hearing unbelievable things. "Well, Mr. Sparks, you know that liability insurance that Mr. Edwards sold you? One of my employees fell off a ladder cleaning the windows and we had to use the policy for compensation. Guess what?" My dad was ready for the punch line. "The insurance policy that we purchased doesn't exist." Panicked, my dad thanked his colleague, dug out his own policy, and started to make phone calls. It didn't take long for him to discover that his own policy wasn't worth the paper it was printed on. Had there been a serious injury, there would have been no coverage in effect. It seems hard for me to believe that these things really happened to my parents. But they did. In this case, we were fortunate. My parents were able to purchase a good policy and get it in effect immediately—before a catastrophe happened.

The Main Idea

The long and short of this chapter is simple: **If you're going to run a business, you're going to have to rely on many different kinds of service people, such as accountants, attorneys, and insurance agents. You can't be too careful in hiring these people. One mistake can cost you the entire business.** Given the mistakes that my parents made in their hiring, they were fortunate to have avoided total devastation.

Chapter 7

Enjoy the Customers—You'll Never Meet a More Eclectic Bunch

No reflection on the doughnut business would be complete without recalling the incredible diversity of customers that walked through our doors over the span of 20 years. If a pollster had used our customers as a sample of all the people on the planet, it seemed to me that the sample would have been highly representative. We saw all kinds. Some of them we were happy to see. Others we could have done without.

For years, an honorable congressman who lived in the same apartment complex as our family did, just two doors down from the doughnut shop, used to start many of his days eating two plain crullers at our doughnut counter while sipping his cup of coffee. He was an impressive individual who stood out in a crowd—every bit the statesman. We felt privileged to have him as a customer.

The Absent-Minded Professor

Actually, we had many educated people who frequented the doughnut shop because we were located close to a major university. But not every educated person was as impressive as our congressman. There was one professor who came in nearly every Saturday morning. We called him Professor

Glasses because the lenses on his glasses were the thickest I'd ever seen. His ritual was always the same. As he came through the door, he was literally dragging two small boys who didn't seem the least bit interested in coming to the doughnut shop. And Professor Glasses didn't seem the least bit interested in the boys. He ordered them a doughnut and juice and then buried his face in a stack of scholarly journal articles. The counter workers hated Professor Glasses because his two boys were totally out of control. After the boys finished their juice, they would jump off their stools and start running around the doughnut shop screaming. Every now and then, Professor Glasses would look up and mutter something to the kids before turning back to his journal articles. This would go on for 45 minutes.

One morning, the kids were being particularly obnoxious and nearly terrorizing the other customers. My brother Dale, who was working the counter at the time, had hit the breaking point. He turned to Professor Glasses to ask him to please take care of his children. To his dismay, when he looked around, he saw that the stool where Professor Glasses had been sitting was now empty. Out of the corner of his eye, he saw Professor Glasses getting into his car in the parking lot. A second later, to Dale's horror, the professor zoomed away, leaving his terrible children to wreak havoc in our doughnut shop, completely unsupervised. Many of the customers sitting at the counter became aware of what had happened. And because they were all familiar with the good professor and his two kids, the incident prompted something of a big group discussion among them. Nearly an hour later, with many of the customers still hanging around to see how the story ended, Professor Glasses came driving back into the parking lot. Sheepishly, he climbed out of his car and came back into the shop. He acknowledged my brother and simply said, "I got too busy reading and forgot that the children were here." After he left the store, dragging the children behind him, a collective roar of laughter went up from the counter as the entire group of customers howled at the professor's behavior. I wish I could have seen the expression on his wife's face when he arrived home with his stack of journals and had to answer the question, "Where are the kids?" From that day on, I never needed to ask what an "absent-minded professor" was. I had just seen a living example.

Mr. Melody and His Unpredictable Son

There weren't many times in the doughnut shop when I felt scared. But one time that I did feel scared was when Mr. Melody came in with his son, Tommy. Mr. Melody worked for a state institution that cared for men and women who at that time were referred to as mentally retarded. Mr. Melody's son was a very large and powerful man in his early twenties, but he had the mental capacity of a 2 - or 3-year-old child. My dad met Mr. Melody when he came calling one day to see if we would sell our day-old doughnuts to the state institution. My dad, being a kind-hearted man, promised Mr. Melody that he would save the old doughnuts for him during the week if they were picked up on Saturday. Mr. Melody was grateful. During the week, we would throw old doughnuts into the empty 50-pound flour bags. By Saturday, we sometimes had two bags completely full. Mr. Melody always came by on Saturday mornings. He would direct Tommy to sit quietly on one of the stools at the counter while he went in the back to collect the old doughnuts. I remember thinking that the state mental institution must really be hard-pressed for funds if they had to rely on my dad's old doughnuts to feed the mentally incapacitated. I didn't like to think about it.

I liked it even less when I was working the doughnut counter and Tommy sat down on a stool while Mr. Melody disappeared into the back of the store. Tommy was loud and often amusing, but usually well-behaved. He always had a rubber ball with him and constantly tossed it in the air and caught it. Unfortunately, his behavior could be unpredictable. Sometimes he would get mad. One morning, Tommy was upset by something and proceeded to rip our newspaper rack away from the window and into the main space where customers walked to their stools. For those few minutes, I thought our doughnut shop had turned into some sort of danger zone. Some of the customers scattered. Others looked on in disbelief. After Mr. Melody managed to calm Tommy and remove him from the store, I sighed in relief. It was one of the few times in my life when I had felt physical danger. One of my colleagues who read my recounting of the story commented in the margin of the page that it made her feel uncomfortable. The comment that I wrote below hers was, "I think I succeeded in capturing the tone of the incident. The people in the store at the time were *really* uncomfortable!"

Another incident occurred a few weeks later when Mr. Melody brought Tommy into the store again. On this occasion, Tommy didn't become angry so much as he became playful. I watched him carefully as he rose from his stool and walked down to the far end of the counter. It was a busy Saturday morning, and each stool was occupied by a customer. Suddenly, Tommy announced that it was time to play "Bop-Bop-Bop." Beginning with the first customer seated at the far end of the store, he raised his powerful arm high into the air over the head of the first poor, befuddled coffee drinker. As he brought his hand down on the head of the customer, he announced at full volume, "Bop." To my dismay, Tommy marched systematically down the line of customers seated at the counter and "bopped" each one on the head. There were men in suits, elderly women who were rather frail, and young children. It didn't matter. Each one received a "bop" on the head from Tommy. As I watched Mr. Melody carry a flour bag of doughnuts in one hand and Tommy's arm in the other as they exited the doughnut shop, I thought I had entered a strange and bizarre world. I don't know if any of the customers who were at the counter that morning ever returned.

Eventually, Mr. Melody had to stop bringing Tommy to the shop. He simply couldn't trust his behavior. After the newspaper-rack incident and the "bopping" episode, I never understood how Mr. Melody trusted Tommy in public for as long as he did. Once, Tommy actually assaulted an innocent customer by whacking him on the back as he stood at the doughnut case selecting his breakfast. On another occasion, he walked back into the kitchen and threw an entire rack of about 45 dozen doughnuts from one end of the kitchen to the other. An innocent worker who had never met Tommy before looked up with a startled expression and said, "What did you do that for, boy?" Tommy didn't speak a word in reply. I think my dad was fortunate that he was never sued for putting customers at risk by allowing Tommy into the store each week. In our current age of knee-jerk litigation, I'm sure that some of these incidents would have triggered many lawsuits if they happened today.

Bert and Ernie in Doughnut Land

Years ago, I stayed in a motel for the weekend with my family, which was part of a tradition that started when my oldest daughter turned 2. Not long after we checked into the motel, I flushed the toilet and noticed that the water was slowly rising to the top of the bowl. In a frantic rush, I tore the cover off the back of the toilet and grabbed the bulb to lift it up. I averted the toilet overflow, but it was still evident that there was a clog. What we needed was a toilet plunger. After hunting around the motel, my father-in-law found a plunger and we were able to unclog the toilet easily. That's when I thought of Bert and Ernie. Not the characters on Sesame

Street—no, our Bert and Ernie were two friends who used to come into the doughnut shop each Saturday morning to enjoy coffee and doughnuts. Their real names were not Bert and Ernie. These were nicknames that the doughnut crew had given them because their physical appearance together somehow reminded us of Bert and Ernie.

Bert was a millionaire, or so I was told. Ernie was not even close to being a millionaire. The two of them had met at our doughnut counter one Saturday morning and had struck up a friendship. Over the years, their appearance became as regular as the brewing of coffee. Frequently, as the family enjoyed a quiet dinner of reflection at the end of a long day, the story of Bert and Ernie would be told. Bert was relatively poor, until he discovered that money could be made in toilet plungers. When he had worked as a clerk in a hardware store, he noticed that the toilet plunger was one of the steady sellers. Using this knowledge, he made some changes to the basic material used in making the handle. He then went to a manufacturer who agreed to make the new handles in bulk and send them to him directly. Of course, the handles had to have plungers on the end, so he ordered them in bulk as well. Then he put together the handles and plungers and became a direct distributor of the new plungers to hardware stores. Eventually, he was taking orders for toilet plungers from hardware stores all around the country, and he filled those orders at a handsome profit for himself. As the story goes, he became a millionaire.

My dad, an engineer and would-be inventor in his own right, loved to tell the story of Bert's success. I think Bert was a hero type for him—he provided inspiration that with a little brain power, financial independence could become a reality. Every time I pick up a toilet plunger today, I think of Bert and the elegant simplicity of his get-rich scheme. Somehow, it never seemed quite right that my family could toil in a doughnut shop for 20 years and walk away with nearly nothing, while Bert simply thought to tinker around with the toilet plunger and achieved financial success. One of the lessons that the doughnut shop taught me at a very young age was to accept your lot in life without asking too many questions. During the doughnut years, I saw people who were vastly better-off than I was (at least I thought they were), and people who were vastly worse-off. It didn't amount to much to ponder the whys and the wherefores. Each Saturday morning, there they were in the flesh: Bert, Mr. Better-Off; and Ernie, Mr. Worse-Off. And they were great friends. Somehow, the two of them seemed to symbolize the fantastic power of coffee and doughnuts to bring together people from very different social spheres.

Derrick—the White-Sheeted Murderer

Probably the most difficult job to fill at the doughnut shop was the job of porter. It seemed like we had a never-ending ad in the newspaper for a person who would agree to mop the floors. I remember one porter, Derrick, who worked for us for only a few months. He was quiet and seemed a little strange. He could frequently be seen wandering around town draped in a white sheet. According to the customer grapevine, Derrick was actually an honor student at the state university and had been voted by his high school class as "most likely to succeed." One of the local attorneys who frequented our store often talked with Derrick as he cleaned the floors around the counter. One day, this attorney remarked to my dad that he would hate to meet up with Derrick as an opposing attorney in the courtroom. I suppose his casual conversations with Derrick had revealed a razor-sharp mind and a quick wit. But in Derrick's case, it was a mind wasted. After I went away to college, I learned that Derrick had fallen in love with a girl from a religious faith that his mother deemed unacceptable. One evening, in a fit of rage over his mother's position, Derrick took a knife and stabbed her to death. After a lengthy trial, Derrick was found innocent on the grounds that he was mentally incompetent. He was assigned to a mental institution. But, amazingly, he was released from the institution after only a few years. We never heard from Derrick again. That was just as well as far as I was concerned. I'm not sure how I would react upon seeing someone who had murdered his own mother. So Derrick may still be out there—wandering some street dressed in a white sheet.

The Tropicanas

For some reason that I never quite understood, the doughnut shop seemed to be a haven for drug traffic and gangs. One gang that used to frequent the shop on weekends called themselves the "Tropicanas." They seemed intent on convincing people that they were mean. One night, they did a great job of convincing my brother Dale and his friend Bob that they were indeed a mean bunch. Bob was back in the kitchen cutting doughnuts out of the dough and occasionally looking through the kitchen window that was right over the baker's table. For some reason, one of the members of the Tropicanas who was drinking coffee at the counter decided that Bob was making faces at him. He rose from his stool and barged his way back into the kitchen while shouting at Bob. He threatened to throw him into the hot fryers. Dale managed to calm the guy down and defuse the situation. The police were called in and no violence was done. But Dale and Bob will never forget the incident. For a little while, it had been terrifying.

Sometimes, when I look back on it, the world of the doughnut shop seems like something out of a dream. But I assure you, in so far as my memory hasn't failed me, all of this happened just as I have told it.

The Main Idea

The simple point in this chapter is that **when you go into business, you ought to be prepared to meet just about anyone.** In the long run, this proved to be great life preparation for me. As a professor at a major university, I see all kinds of students. But as diverse as the college campus is, it can't hold a candle to the diversity of the doughnut shop. From U.S. congressmen to crazy murderers, going into business is a ticket for meeting all varieties of sinners and saints.

Chapter 8

Know the Parent Company: Some Parents Are Better Than Others

It's possible that my parents' experience with their franchise was unusual, but I doubt it. Still, I don't necessarily advise people away from franchise arrangements, but I do encourage would-be franchise operators to think very carefully about the relationship that they might enter into when they take on the name of a parent company.

In the case of my parents, the relationship that they had with the parent company was less than harmonious. In preparing to write this book, I did some research on the nature of franchise systems in the 1960s. Over and over again, I found writers pointing out that some personalities were simply not cut out for the franchise arrangement. My parents were probably too independent-minded to really get along well with a parent company. They were like rebellious adolescents who believed that they could do better on their own. Whether they really could have done better is a question that will never be answered. Part of the problem with franchising is that it can be easy for the franchisee to come to the belief that the parent company is getting too much money (a percentage of the store's gross sales) for not doing any work. It's easy to forget that the parent company provides the name, advertising, and a system that is supposed to keep the franchisee from having to start from scratch. The parent company puts a lot of work into the front end of the operation to get the franchisee ready for business. My parents had to go away to train for several weeks. But once a person starts running the business, he or she might tend to minimize the importance of that front-end work. In any case, if you are contemplating a franchise, one area to investigate very carefully is the relationship with the parent company. In my parents' case, they certainly didn't end up regarding the company as their best friend.

Problems from the Very Beginning

When I've listened to my parents tell the story of their opening, it's hard to believe that they didn't raise more serious questions to themselves about their ability to get along well with the parent company prior to signing the contract. According to my folks, the parent company was to arrange for them to have a store in a town that was just a few miles from our home. My parents made arrangements to rent a house that would have been adjacent to the new store. But out of the blue, according to my parents, a company salesman informed them that the store had fallen through at that location. Not long after receiving this news, they drove by the location where the store had been planned and saw a huge sign announcing the coming of their company's doughnut shop. They were perplexed. They discovered that the company had decided to give that store to another local operator who wanted a second store. Who knows what factors may have been operating here. Perhaps the company's behavior was entirely justified and my parents simply failed to see the big picture full of all the details that a large company had to manage. Whatever the case, from my parents' perspective, this was not the most satisfying way to start off the relationship. My parents had the sense that there was a much bigger game being played than the one that they were trying to play. But they felt that since the game had begun, they couldn't back out. And they didn't.

After losing the chance to own a store in their hometown, my parents were given a choice to wait indefinitely for another opportunity in their home area, or move 150 miles away to another state to open a store in a matter of months. After careful deliberation, they decided to move. The dream of owning their own business, even if it was three hours away from home, was just too compelling. My brothers and I were sent off to a summer camp while my parents prepared for the opening of the store. It was an odd feeling to leave our lifelong home for camp and return to a strange place that was now called home. Looking back, I am sure that the many dislocated relationships that were left in the wake of our move contributed to the stress that the family felt during the first year or two. Nevertheless, we managed to cope.

The plan was that the store would open during the last week of May. In the last part of April and the beginning of May, my parents ran newspaper ads to recruit employees. A number of high school students who wanted summer jobs applied for work and my parents lined up their schedule. In mid-May, however, my parents noticed that the construction workers who had been reporting daily to work on the store were no longer coming. The store sat unfinished. When my parents inquired as to the delay, they discovered that the crew was working on another store about 40 miles away. They had no control over this situation at all. My parents waited around for many weeks. Finally, their store opened for business in late July. But many of the high school students who had originally been scheduled to work at the end of May had taken other summer jobs. Covering the opening shifts was a major problem. To make matters worse, my parents had signed a contract that obligated them to pay their building rent and equipment rent on the first of the month. After being open for less than a week, they had to shell out two major payments. As the month of August arrived, my parents were well on their way to being in debt. Perhaps none of this could have been avoided and no one was really to blame. But my parents didn't feel too good about their new business venture from the very beginning.

Advice from the Parent Company

The only thing my parents knew about the doughnut business was what the company told them. Sometimes, it seemed to them that what the company told them didn't work out very well. This may not have been the fault of the company. Perhaps their advice had worked well at other stores, but it just didn't seem to work for my folks. For example, my parents were told to hire a certain number of workers on each shift just to handle the counter trade. After a few days, my parents realized that for their situation, the number they had been given was entirely too many. There simply wasn't enough work for all of them. But the company representatives insisted that once business picked up after the opening, we would need every single one of the workers we had hired. So my parents stayed with the suggested number for a while longer. Finally, unable to wait any longer, they cut their counter staff dramatically—contrary to company advice. Prior to this move, their payroll was 300 percent higher than it needed to be. One of the reasons that my brothers and I saw so little of my parents during the opening weeks of business was because they believed that they had to be there to staff the counter if it was understaffed. Gradually, they realized that far fewer workers were really needed for their store.

Company advice was given regarding doughnut production, too. The company counseled my parents to make doughnuts around the clock—resulting in triple the amount of doughnuts that were being sold on a daily basis. Again, upon having to throw out nearly 70 percent of the production each day, my parents quickly got wise to the fact that the company's advice was not best in their case. Perhaps the company's wisdom was tried-and-true at other stores and represented their best guess at what would happen at our store. Nevertheless, my parents' discovery that the company's advice didn't always work out had a dampening effect on the respect, warmth, and affection that they felt for the company representatives who supposedly had their best interests at heart.

Vicious Rumors

After spiraling into debt to the tune of $15,000 in the first three months of operation (equivalent to over $100,000 in today's currency), my parents invested every ounce of their energy into saving their investment. They were as baffled about what had happened as they were tired of the long shifts and all-nighters they endured at the doughnut shop. During this time period, my parents talked to many other people in the business, some of whom were also franchise operators. One of the things that they heard was unbelievable. According to the views of some, the advice that my parents had received from the company might have been calculated. According to this incredible theory, if after just a few months my parents lost so much money that they went bankrupt, the company could come in and assume the daily operation of the store for a short time, and then sell the store all over again to a new investor. The customer would hardly notice the change in ownership. If the company could continue to do this, they might be able to resell the same store multiple times. If something like this was actually happening, it would have been a scam, plain and simple. For my parents, choosing to believe this outrageous scenario actually became a strong temptation in order to explain the near bankrupt situation that they found themselves in after just a few months of being in business.

Looking back on it, however, I would like to believe that such stories about company strategy to resell doughnut shops were just vicious rumors. At the time, trying to figure out whether there was any truth to these stories and whether they accounted for the early problems my parents had was impossible. Now, several decades later, when memories of the facts are blurry and uncertain, it is even *less* possible. Still, with this sort of rumor floating around, my parents undoubtedly adopted an attitude of caution in dealing with the company. That was probably wise. As my parents tell the story, the parent company actually had control over the business' books for the first few months. To me, it has always seemed beyond belief that my parents were not even keeping their own books when the business opened. That fact was a symptom of their trust in the parent company. As things progressed, my parents certainly wondered about whether that trust had been misplaced or not.

Milk for the Construction Workers?

The parent company had advised that my parents permit them to keep the books on the business for the first few months until the shop was running smoothly. But as the financial reports from the company began to look bleaker and bleaker, my parents made the move to take personal control over their books. When they obtained control, they hired their own accountant to scrutinize the financial picture of the first few months. The accountant immediately discovered several curious entries.

In one case, the books showed that my parents had paid a bill for $2,500 to the milk company for an order that had been delivered to the store in April. Considering that the store didn't open until late July, there were only a few possibilities. The first was that the milk company delivered all of this milk to the construction workers who ended up consuming it before it went bad. Not likely. The construction workers preferred beer. And in any case, generous as they were, my parents certainly didn't authorize the milk company to supply the construction workers with milk. Another possibility was that the parent company had created a phony bill in order to take $2,500 from my parents' business. To my parents, this sounded even more fantastic than the first option. A third possibility was that there had been an accidental entry—perhaps confusing another store's records with the records of our store. One thing was certain upon discovering the entry: my parents decided to keep the books in the hands of their personal accountant. Too much time has passed for me to know for sure whether this switch proved to be immediately helpful. At the very least, my parents managed to stay in business.

Paying to Clean Other People's Aprons?

Another irregularity in the books was a bill that my parents supposedly had paid to clean dirty aprons. In the doughnut shop, aprons get dirty fast. There is really nothing that smells more offensive than a baker's apron after a full shift of producing doughnuts. You might think that the aroma would be sweet, like fresh bread. Not at all. After the aprons were taken off and stored in a closed container for only a day, they smelled like a weird mix of things that most resembled strong vinegar. I'm sure that a chemist could explain why. In any case, clean aprons were essential each day in the doughnut shop and the only way to make this happen was to hire a linen service. Every Thursday, dirty aprons were collected and fresh aprons were returned. My parents gladly paid their linen bill. But when the company turned over the books, it appeared as if my parents had paid a linen bill of several hundred dollars for another doughnut store that was located in different region of the state. Upon making this discovery, their faith in the company's good will and friendly advice took another hit. They also discovered that they had paid thousands of dollars for cans of doughnut filling, flour, and various other products that had never been delivered to their store. Were these entries in the books just innocent, routine mistakes that happened all the time in business accounting? Maybe so, maybe not. By this time, my parents had learned to be wary, just in case anyone tried to take advantage of them. It was a stunning lesson. My parents had never been required to think this way in their entire lives. It revolutionized their entire worldview. I never learned very much about the questions my parents might have asked the folks at the parent company about these sorts of issues. I always had the impression that if they did ask questions, the answers they got never resulted in any monetary adjustments in their favor. Eventually, my parents worked their way out of debt and held on to their store through grit and determination. As it turned out, the business was great at bringing in cash. To my knowledge, my parents never revisited any of the discrepancies in the bookkeeping in an attempt to resolve them. When I reflect today on what seems to me to be incredibly sloppy accounting practice, I marvel that anyone managed to do any accurate accounting when it came to the doughnut shop. Records that would be placed with ease today on a Microsoft Excel spreadsheet had to be handwritten on long ledger pages back when I was a kid. It's amazing that that any accurate records were kept at all.

The Big Doughnut Giveaway

The parent company was particularly "helpful" in promoting doughnut sales. Shortly after our business opened, a customer appeared at the doughnut counter one Friday evening with a coupon that she had clipped from the afternoon newspaper. The coupon entitled the holder to a half-dozen free doughnuts with the purchase of a dozen. My parents examined the coupon carefully and honored it. But they were somewhat concerned. They had known nothing about this promotion and were hardly ready to meet the demand that was about to be placed on the doughnut supply.

In a matter of hours, it was clear that we had a doughnut emergency on our hands. We were making doughnuts as fast as we could, but we simply couldn't keep up with the demand. At the peak of the crisis, we were actually purchasing unfinished doughnuts from another store in the area just to keep our supply intact. This seemed stupid. We were buying doughnuts to give them away for free. But the negative repercussions of turning customers away who expected a free half-dozen were unthinkable. We had to do it. In the middle of this debacle, my dad and Felipe were doing double-duty in the kitchen, baking as many doughnuts as two men could. But before the doughnuts could be finished and put out on the display cases to sell, they had to cool. Since time was of the essence, my dad, still an engineer at heart, got the idea of hoisting an entire rack of doughnuts into the air to allow them to receive the direct airflow produced by the kitchen exhaust fan. (Remember the ten kites?) Felipe hoisted one side of the rack and my dad hoisted the other. Unfortunately, they didn't hoist the rack at the same rate. Felipe hoisted his end much faster and the top of the rack zoomed up toward the ceiling where it smashed into two florescent lights. Glass shattered everywhere, all over the rack of doughnuts and into the deep-frying vats that contained over 300 pounds of shortening. This was one of those times when all one can do is laugh. And that is exactly what my father and Felipe did. It took a long time to clean up the mess, and all of the doughnuts had to be discarded. In the meantime, we increased the order for unfinished doughnuts to the other stores in the area. Fortunately, the coupon offer expired at the end of the weekend. But when the final damage was calculated, my parents had spent close to $1,000 on doughnuts that were given away free. Who knows if the goodwill we earned ever came back to us in the form of repeat sales? I think my parents would say that it didn't. They never liked the doughnut giveaways that the parent company sponsored on their behalf.

Changing the Rules in the Middle of the Game

One story that was constantly repeated to family and friends during the doughnut years was one that I found hard to comprehend. Having never seen the contract that my parents signed with the company, I can't say for sure whether the story I heard was true in every detail. But I have no real reason to doubt it. Apparently, when my parents opened their store, they signed a contract that called for them to pay the company a small percentage of their total gross sales. This percentage was to pay for advertising that the company ran in the local and national media, plus a general franchise charge. A few years after my parents started the business, the parent company notified them that their new contracts with franchise operators called for a higher percentage of the gross to go into the company's pockets. They insisted that my parents comply with the new contract, even though this was not what the original contract had specified. After some legal battles, my parents decided that it was better to relent and sign the new agreement. I think my parents probably needed a better attorney.

In another example of what seemed like a change in the ground rules, after promising my parents that another doughnut shop under the company name would not open within a 10-mile radius of their store, they promptly opened one about 2 miles up the road—on the very same street. Fortunately, it didn't seem to hurt business. But my parents quickly learned to evaluate the word of the company with a good deal of care.

Baker Shenanigans

A supervisor from the parent company is supposed to help the franchise operator manage a better business. In our case, it was difficult to know just how well these supervisors did their jobs. On one occasion, my parents were forced to decide between the presumed goodwill of the parent company and the credibility of one of their bakers from Costa Rica. According to the baker, Felipe, a supervisor entered our store one day and asked him to join him for a cup of coffee. Felipe claimed that the supervisor told him that my parents had sold their store and that he would be out of a job by the end of the week. Felipe also claimed that the supervisor then offered him another baker's job at a company-run store somewhere else in the region. Whether the story about the supervisor was true or whether Felipe invented it to justify his wanderlust is hard to determine. He was a very shy man and he did take a job at another store without ever saying a word to my parents. For six weeks, my dad was the full-time baker. Finally, one day, Felipe returned to the store to pick up his last paycheck. My father asked Felipe what in the world had happened. He offered Felipe his old job back if he would tell him the truth. Felipe poured out the tale of how the supervisor had convinced him that our store had been sold. Apparently, Felipe much preferred working for my dad and was glad to come back.

If Felipe's story was only a convenient fiction, then what happened to the company supervisor a few weeks later was truly a travesty. As my dad told the story, the supervisor showed up on a routine visit to the store and ordered a cup of coffee. When my dad spotted him, he also noticed that there was a local police officer in the store. In a volume that could be heard by every customer in the store, my dad went out and asked the police officer, "Sir, would you please escort this man off of these premises before the two of us go 'loop-deloop' all over the parking lot?" I don't think the supervisor had ever heard anything like that in his life. The officer complied and the supervisor left quickly, never to return again. From that day on, we were probably the only store in the state that never received a visit from the supervisor. My parents never expressed any disappointment about that.

Months later, my parents heard that this same supervisor had actually bought his own store from the parent company and attempted to embezzle them out of huge amounts of cash. We also heard that the parent company got wise and brought him to court. Before they could remove him from the store, he died of a heart attack. Sometimes, the doughnut business seemed like a war, complete with all the casualties.

The Parent Company Will Usually Win in the End

Unless you have a good attorney with unusual skill (something that I clearly recommend), and enough money to pay the legal bills, it is unlikely that you can beat the company in many legal disputes. Generally speaking, the parent company got its way. Maybe this is just how franchises are supposed to work. My parents never completely adjusted to this reality.

When my parents decided after about 14 years that they wanted out of the doughnut business before their 20-year contract expired, they looked for a private party to sell to. This was supposed to be entirely possible under their contract with the parent company. But my parents' attempts to sell their store seemed ill-fated from the beginning.

When the store was opened, the company's opening crew had set up a newspaper stand and a milk machine that contained quarts of milk for sale to the customers. For some reason that my parents never could understand, years and years after our store had operated with these amenities, the company issued an edict that the milk machine and newspaper stand had to go. My parents refused to do this because they believed that these two items had become staples of the business that our customers appreciated. The parent company took my parents to court in an attempt to force them to do away with the milk and newspapers. This always seemed like a silly legal battle to my parents. It may have been silly, but it also turned out to be serious. It wasn't until they tried to sell their store to a private party that they discovered a terrible rude fact: their store could not be sold while litigation was pending. Was this a purposeful strategy by the parent company to prevent my parents from selling their franchise? We'll never know for sure.

After the litigation ended (in my parents' favor), my parents noticed that there was a pattern taking place with prospective buyers. We never heard from them again after they talked to the parent company. So my dad decided to play detective. In the case of one interested buyer, he asked if the person would be so kind as to contact the parent company on our store telephone and permit my parents to listen to the call on the extension. The potential buyer agreed. My dad wondered until the day he died if he heard the conversation correctly. As he recalled it, he heard the company representative tell our prospective buyer that our store had already been sold to someone else and that there was another store he could buy from them if he was interested. I suppose it was possible that this company representative really believed that our store had already been sold. But, in fact, it hadn't been. It is also possible that the parent company knew nothing about the rogue actions of one representative who was out of line. Reportedly, this particular representative died just a few years later so I guess we'll never know. It didn't matter. The prospective buyer was undoubtedly put off by hearing different accounts about the status of the store from my dad and the company representative. He must have gotten cold feet and any prospect for a sale was lost.

By the time my parents finally left the business, their suspicions had also been raised about several other things that happened during that period of time. One morning, we received a phone call at home from one of the counter workers informing us that there were union members walking back and forth across the entrance to the store. They were holding picket signs and were supposedly protesting the fact that my parents' employees were not unionized. While they did hurt the business for the two-week period they were there, my parents could never quite figure out where they came from or why they were there. None of the employees wanted a union. A high percentage of the employees were high-school students who worked a few hours after school. What was going on? After a while, it seemed to me that the parent company became a convenient scapegoat for almost anything that went wrong in our business. While this was understandable from the perspective of human psychology, it probably wasn't fair to the company.

At the end of my parents' 20 years in the doughnut business, the parent company refused to refranchise them for a second term. As I recall it, their reason for refusing was that my parents did not want to remodel their store to conform to the new building design on new stores going up around the country. It wasn't that my parents didn't like the new design or didn't want it. It was simply the fact that it would have cost them $130,000 to remodel. My parents' attorney wanted to file a $1 million lawsuit against the parent company for their refusal to refranchise my parents. He said we had an excellent chance of winning. But he wanted $25,000 up front. My parents eventually decided that they didn't want to risk any more money in disputes with the parent company, so they decided to walk away rather than fight. My mom always declared that it was the best decision they ever made. I think my dad went to his grave with some regrets. He was a fighter and he hated to lose. Even though he probably felt that the company had beaten him in the end, I think he walked away a winner. After leaving the business, he never had to go to bed wondering if a 5:30 a.m. phone call would signal him to roll out of bed and report for baker duty.

The Main Idea

If you're contemplating a franchise-type business, investigate the parent company carefully. Consistent with the theme of doing plenty of research before going into business, the prospective franchise operator should do some field research. **Talk to others who have ventured into the franchise agreement. Then try to actually go to work in the business for a trial period of at least six months before making a decision to take the plunge.**

And when talking to other franchise operators about the parent company, it would pay to be a bit less oblique than my dad was on one occasion. I will never forget the time that we went into another doughnut shop in another state that had the same company sign as our store's. My dad introduced himself to the owner and asked him, "How do you get along with the men on the sign?" His question was met with a blank stare, and then the soft-spoken owner asked my dad to repeat his question. "What do you think of the men on the sign?" my dad asked. A look of concern crossed the owner's face as he rushed outside to look at his sign. He thought that my dad had spotted some men high up in the air, climbing around on his sign. Not that something so bizarre as men climbing on your sign couldn't have happened. But in this case, my dad was simply using a figure of speech that completely befuddled his fellow franchise operator. My dad probably should have used a more direct question like, "How do you get along with the parent company?"

Chapter 9

A Kaleidoscope of Little Memories—Like Icing on a Cake Doughnut

I'm now letting my mind roam freely over the period of running the doughnut shop in order to capture memories that were not right at the surface. These stories convey significance to me about the nature of growing up in a family business. I'm sure that my brothers and parents would all have a different list of memories. In the end, the point I want to convey is that **running a business is not just a financial endeavor. It is a life experience with highs, lows, joys, and reservations.**

Playing Games with the Telephone

A few years into the business operation, my parents were growing increasingly frustrated with the fact that whenever they were away from the doughnut shop, they missed important phone calls. Moreover, my dad would often discover that when he entered the shop unexpectedly, some of the counter help was back in the kitchen on the phone with a friend instead of filling the napkin dispensers or replenishing the coffee supply. This situation called for action. After a few inquiries with the phone company, my parents discovered that they could get an extension to the doughnut shop telephone placed in our home. In addition, the extension could be outfitted with a switch that would cut the phone off at the doughnut shop and leave the line open at the residence. A speaker attached to the phone would allow my parents to monitor the phone calls that came to the doughnut shop. This high technology seemed too good to be true. My parents ordered it instantly.

Like much new technology, the phone extension to the doughnut shop was a blessing and a curse. Occasionally, my parents were able to monitor phone calls, and when important ones came in, they would pick up the phone and announce that they would take the call. Sometimes, this baffled the counter help who had initially answered the phone. If they were new, they may not have known that my parents could answer the phone at their home. When my parents would break into the call, the employees would often express surprise that my parents were at the shop. Usually, they would discover in short order that there was an extension at my parents' home. And this certainly did cut down on personal phone calls during work hours. Sometimes, when an employee used the phone to make a personal call, my mom would simply throw the switch that closed the line down at the shop. The employees got the message quickly that the business phone wasn't available for personal calls.

Unfortunately, the phone extension had two distinct disadvantages. The first was that whenever the phone rang in the doughnut shop, it also rang in our house. I can assure you that the doughnut shop received at least 10 to 20 times the number of phone calls that we received on our home phone. What made this especially irritating at the beginning was that my parents felt compelled to halt all conversation and activity in the house whenever the business phone rang in order to monitor the call. Since the home phone and doughnut shop phone were adjacently mounted on our kitchen wall, it was nearly impossible to tell which one was ringing. Sometimes they both rang together. This didn't exactly contribute to a peaceful home environment. There were times when I wasn't sure whether I was home or at the doughnut shop. Listening to people place advance orders for doughnuts while sitting in my living room wore thin quickly. The second disadvantage was that, often, when my parents threw the switch that closed down the line at the doughnut shop, they forgot to switch it back. Sometimes, when nobody was home to realize this fact, the doughnut shop would go for hours and hours without receiving any phone calls. And of course, no one in the shop could call out either. I remember sometimes having to walk home from the shop to tell my parents to turn the phone back on. As I think back on it, all of the bother with the phone extension created more problems than it solved. I don't know if my parents would have agreed or not.

Doughnuts and Fish & Chips Don't Go Together

When my dad decided to move from doughnut routes to a doughnut shop, he was caught up in the principle that bigger would be better. Amazingly, even after all of the struggles of the first years of the doughnut business, this principle was still alive and kicking in my dad's mind. Unbelievably, he contracted with a well-known fish & chips franchise company and opened a fish & chips restaurant about seven blocks down the street from the doughnut shop. The idea was that my brother Wayne would become the manager of this store and make it his livelihood. But the adventure with fish & chips began with a minor calamity. After my parents had paid the fish & chips company to get their kitchen equipment, they read in the newspaper that the company had filed for bankruptcy. The kitchen equipment never arrived and the money they had paid for it was gone forever. They had to buy the equipment again—this time directly from the supplier. It was the most expensive kitchen ever installed in a fish & chips restaurant. The upside of the bankruptcy was that it meant that a number of the standard fees that would normally be paid to the parent company would not have to be paid once the restaurant opened. There was no parent company to receive any money.

Initially, the fish & chips business did well. But gradually, for whatever reasons, business tailed off. The product was good but service may have been a bit slow, and the ethnic makeup of the area just didn't seem conducive to fried and battered fish. People preferred to eat bagels or pizza. The fish & chips experiment was failing fast.

My parents thought that one reason for the failing business was the fact that the town enforced a strict sign ordinance that prevented them from having the sign they thought they needed. It was a question of having signs at the proper angles to the passing traffic. After the town made its ruling, my dad decided to use my automobile that I had left behind when I went to college for a novel purpose. He backed the car up to the street at the proper angle, opened the trunk, and propped up a large wooden sign that he had made to advertise the daily specials. It didn't work. The town immediately ruled the sign illegal. My dad was defiant, even in the wake of $100 per day fines from the court. Finally, with no help from his high-priced attorney, he had the fines waived after agreeing to remove the unsightly sign perched on the rear of my car. Business continued to drop steadily.

When business owners find themselves in financial crisis, all sorts of ideas begin to surface. As manager of the fish & chips store, Wayne recalled a story that my parents had told him a few years earlier about a man who we nicknamed "Sammy the Torch."

"Sammy the Torch" operated a doughnut shop just like my parents'. But unlike my parents' shop, his was losing money. Sammy decided that he needed a way out. His overnight profits had become so low that he decided to start closing the store in the evening and reopening in the morning. On one particular evening, he had an inspiration after saying goodbye to the last employee who left for home—a middle-aged woman who had been serving coffee to the few stray customers. After he was certain that she had departed, Sammy locked the doors and went over to the deep vats of shortening in the doughnut fryer. He lifted one of the heating elements out of the fryer and tied a rope around it. He connected the other end of the rope to the kitchen ceiling. Just before he left, he turned on the heating element. He reasoned that the rope would catch fire and the store would burn. He would collect insurance for the loss and his financial situation would be saved.

My parents heard the news that Sammy's store had burned down and wondered exactly what had happened. About a year later, they happened to see Sammy in a shopping mall and took the opportunity to chat. Sammy told them the story, filling in the details. As he had left the store that night, he saw, to his horror, that the employee who had left the store just before him was standing out front on the street waiting for a bus. When Sammy glanced back at the store and saw the glow of flames in the kitchen, he quickly offered the woman a ride home. Fortunately for him, she accepted the ride readily because it had grown cold waiting for the bus. After Sammy dropped her off at her home, he went to his own house and arrived just in time to receive a phone call from the police telling him that his store was on fire. He rushed back to the store and remained on the scene until the fire was extinguished.

The store was damaged so badly that it was a complete loss. Sammy told my parents that as the firemen were still walking around the premises, he looked over and saw a corner of the fryer heating element sticking up out of the fryer where it had dropped from the rope that had suspended it earlier.

In the chaos and commotion of the fire's aftermath, Sammy backed up to the fryer so no one could see what he was doing and he gently lifted the heating element so that it once again slid back into place at the bottom of the fryer. Apparently, his deed was never discovered and his plan had actually worked. After watching so many episodes of *CSI*, I can only assume that the investigative techniques for arson at the time of this incident were primitive by today's standards.

Possibly under the inspiration of "Sammy the Torch," my brother Wayne proved that old habits die hard. In an insightful lyric, master songwriter Paul Simon once wrote, "After changes upon changes, we are more or less the same." Certainly that seemed to be the case when it came to Wayne. Just as he had opted out of the doughnut routes when he was a boy by throwing his doughnuts down the sewer, Wayne decided that a quick exit from the fish & chips business would also be the ticket to freedom. As it happened, we lived right down the street from the fish & chips restaurant. One could walk door-to-door in about three minutes. If you ran, you could make it in a minute. This close proximity may have helped give Wayne an idea.

One summer night, with the business failing miserably and no good escape plan in sight, Wayne decided in a stroke of stupidity that he would burn the restaurant down and hope that the insurance money would bail us out of a bad situation. He knew that if he told my dad about his plan, all hell would break loose. My dad wouldn't go for anything like that under any circumstances. So Wayne proceeded without my dad's blessing. His plan was that my dad would never discover that it was arson, and everything would turn out OK in the end. What Wayne didn't know was that just a week earlier, my parents had taken a dramatic cost-cutting move and dropped their fire insurance on the fish & chips restaurant in order to keep the business alive awhile longer.

Late one night, at about 2 a.m., Wayne prepared to leave the restaurant. The last thing he did was soak his small office just off the kitchen with gasoline. Leaving the office door wide open (it was a regular hinged door, not on a spring of any kind), he lit the fuel with a match. As he closed the back door of the restaurant behind him, the last thing he saw was the office in full blaze. He quickly locked the back door and dashed down the street. Heart pounding, he quietly entered the house and made his way to his bedroom. In a matter of minutes, he was safely tucked away under the sheets. He clutched the sheets and waited for the sirens. At first he thought he must be in some sort of a time warp. It had seemed like hours since he jumped into bed, but he knew it had only been minutes. Still no sirens. He waited…and waited. Nothing. At 6 a.m. the sun came up, but the sirens never came. Wayne's curiosity was too much to bear. Usually, he went to the restaurant at about 10 a.m. to begin preparations for opening at 11 for lunch. But on this morning, he was up before anyone else and out of the house before breakfast. As he neared the restaurant, e could see that it was still standing, with no sign of damage. What had happened? Slowly, he opened the back door and was greeted with a faint smell of smoke. As he walked in, he stared in disbelief. His office door, which had been standing wide open when he left the restaurant, was shut tight as a drum. He walked over and opened the office door. What he saw defied the imagination. There were a few papers on the floor with burn marks on them, but other than that, there was literally no evidence that there had been a fire. Given the way the flames had been raging upon his departure, Wayne simply couldn't comprehend how this could be. Of course, he had to explain the smell of smoke and fuel to my parents when they arrived later that morning. He confessed everything, and my dad had the predictable fit. But overall, the biggest emotion was relief. Having to cut their financial losses and close the business (which is what they did shortly after this episode) was much better than serving a prison term for arson.

Wayne has one theory about what may have happened that night. Possibly, when he closed the large back door upon leaving the restaurant, the rush of air into the kitchen caught the office door and slammed it shut...depriving the fire of needed oxygen. It always sounded like a good theory to me. Fire departments routinely try to get the word out that the best defense against a fire is to simply close the door before you leave a building that might be ablaze. But when Wayne reflects today about this possibility, he ultimately rejects it. He says he just can't figure out how there was so little damage from the raging fire that he saw with his own eyes. And he really isn't convinced that closing the one outside door could have created enough of a wind at the right angle to close the inside office door. He tried to replicate that effect over and over without success. His own conclusion all these years later is that God closed that office door. Today, Wayne is fervent about his belief in God. Perhaps his spiritual journey started on the night when he discovered that he couldn't burn down a building if he tried. The rest of the family is glad that he couldn't.

Like a Bridge Over Troubled Water

One of the more amusing incidents that I remember from the doughnut shop happened on a Friday night. My dad had been approached by some young teens from his church earlier in the week, asking him if it would be OK to come to the doughnut shop on Friday evening and talk to people over coffee about their spiritual welfare. Not wanting to discourage these young people and reasoning that he couldn't keep them from coming in and talking about anything they wanted, my dad consented after warning them about not bothering his customers or getting into heated arguments.

One reason he was concerned about the possibility of arguments was because the overwhelming majority of the residents of our town were Jewish. He knew that the teens would be interested in talking about Christianity. So even after consenting to the arrangement, my dad was a little anxious about not offending his customers. I think the only reason he gave the go-ahead to the teens was because they looked fairly innocent and he wanted to be nice. Just to make sure that things were not going to get out of hand, my dad decided to take a pass by the doughnut shop about 45 minutes after he knew the teens were planning to start their conversations over coffee. When he drove his car into the parking lot, nothing could have prepared him for what he saw. In the main corner window of the store, which ran from the floor to the ceiling, was a huge colorful sign with a bright rainbow. Slowly, my dad stared at the large blue letters that were painted on the sign and read the words aloud incredulously: "Jesus—Like a Bridge Over Troubled Water—Come In and Let's Talk about Christ." I don't think I've ever seen my dad move faster. Before I could even get my car door open, he was inside the store, trying to wipe off a cold sweat from his brow with one hand while dismantling the sign with the other. He gently called the teens into the back kitchen and explained that talking was one thing, but they were not going to be permitted to turn his doughnut shop into a religious coffeehouse. We'll never know how many Jewish customers walked away from our store that night wondering whether the rabbi would approve of buying doughnuts from a store advertising discussions about Christ. I don't remember any serious fallout from this incident, but my dad never gave the kids another chance to test the theory that the sign would result in decreased sales.

Learning to Fix Air Conditioners

In the summertime, it was absolutely essential to have the doughnut shop fully air-conditioned. The kitchen got hot due to the large vats of hot grease. And if temperatures really soared, the sugar on the doughnuts would become moist and start to melt. Not to mention that the employees would become increasingly irritable.

One day in late June, during the first really hot summer of operation, the air conditioner stopped working. My dad called a repairman who promptly came out, climbed a ladder to the roof, and came back down in just a few minutes. The cool air came pumping out of the vents again and we were in business. The repair bill was $35. The only problem was that the air conditioner went out again the following day. Another call to the repairman. Once again, he climbed a ladder to the roof and came down quickly. The air conditioner was fixed again. Another bill for $35. My dad inquired about the problem and the repairman said that on these hot days, a unit like ours would frequently need "adjusting" and that there was nothing he could do to avoid these repair bills during the hot weather. Sure enough, the next day, the unit stopped functioning again and my dad called the repairman a third time. This time when he arrived, my dad climbed the ladder too and announced that he wanted to see what kind of "adjustment" needed to be made. To my dad's shock, the repairman leaned down and placed his finger over a red button that had the word "reset" printed on the surface. Immediately after he pushed it, the unit began to run again. "Is that all you've been doing each time you charged me $35," asked my dad incredulously. "That's all there is to it," said the repairman. "That will be $35, Mr. Sparks." From that point on, I made many treks up that ladder on hot summer days to push the reset button. I asked my dad if I could have just a portion of the $35 that he was saving each time I did it. I was never able to collect.

The Plumbing Nightmare

We will never forget the most horrendous plumbing problem we had that defied the imagination. It wasn't one that could be easily repaired with Bert's toilet plunger. One very cold winter day, one of our bakers (Eddy), was assigned the job of filtering the fryers at the end of his shift. This was not a task that the bakers enjoyed doing. But it had to be done at least once each week in order to keep the shortening pure. Eddy was in a hurry to leave on this particular day and decided that instead of running the shortening through the filtering machine, it would be faster to use the machine to direct the liquid shortening down the kitchen drain. He would simply add all new shortening to the fryers and be done with it.

Shortly after the shortening went down the drain, every plumbing system in the store started to back up. Plumbers were called in with wire snakes to unclog the drains. They couldn't do it. As the 300 pounds of liquid shortening made its way through the pipes under the parking lot, the cold winter temperature took its toll. The shortening froze. In the end, the concrete parking lot had to be dug up in order to gain access to the main pipes. It was the messiest thing I had ever seen. Needless to say, we received one gigantic bill from the plumbers.

Vinney—the Sunday Baker

A few years after we opened the doughnut shop, a short, tough-looking Italian man showed up at the doughnut shop and asked my dad if he needed a baker on Sundays. Vinney was a truck driver. But he was in need of extra cash and begged for a break. Somewhere along the line, he had learned how to make doughnuts and my dad decided to try him out. Before we went into business, we had usually gone to church on Sundays. But the first few years of the doughnut business were far too unpredictable to mount any kind of steady church attendance. Hiring Vinney would afford us more of an opportunity to return to Sunday services. Vinney turned out to be a good hire. For nearly 15 years, he never missed a Sunday. He was the most reliable employee we ever hired.

Often, I would work early on Sunday mornings as the doughnut finisher while Vinney baked the doughnuts. Vinney liked to start early, so I was able to complete the job by 10:30 a.m. and then rush home in an attempt to get to church on time. Vinney was hard to dislike, although he was clearly one of the crudest men I had ever met. When the young high school girls would walk through the kitchen on their break, Vinney would walk up to them and say things like, "If I told you that your body was beautiful, would you hold it against me?" In today's workplace environment, Vinney would be fired in a minute for sexual harassment. He probably would have been sued as well. Spending the early part of Sunday morning working with Vinney and the latter part in a worship service often made me feel like I had one foot in heaven and one foot in hell.

Every Vehicle Should Carry a Doughnut Screen

I always liked the mechanics of making doughnuts. Three dozen wads of dough were placed neatly on large wire screens. In the case of yeast doughnuts (the kind you fill with jelly), the screens were placed on a large rack that was wheeled into a large, enclosed space that had a single burner under a pot of water. The idea was that the water produced steam and the humid air in the box helped the yeast dough to puff up so the doughnuts were ready to fry. In the doughnut trade, this box was referred to as a "proof box." When the yeast doughnuts were puffed up high enough, the rack would be wheeled out next to the fryers. Using some metal handles that fit around the edges of the screen, each set of 36 doughnuts was lowered into a large vat of hot oil where they fried quickly. The handles actually remained attached to the screens and stuck out about eight inches over the surface of the oil. When the doughnuts were fried, the screen was lifted up through the oil to catch the doughnuts that were floating on the surface. When I first learned how to fry the doughnuts, I couldn't comprehend how one held on to the metal handles after they had been lowered into the oil. They conducted heat very well and the tops of the handles were often too hot to grip, at least for me. I was informed by my dad that you simply had to bear the pain. After the screen was lifted out of the oil, it was set aside to allow the doughnuts to drain and cool. One would think that these wire screens were only good for frying doughnuts. But one day, many people in the town discovered that doughnut screens were good for something else.

It was a cold January day and a strong winter snowstorm moved in at about 3 a.m. By 7 a.m., the roads were so slick that schools were closed. The forecast was for a major storm. The regular bakers didn't make it to work that day so my dad was the baker. Since school was closed, I ended up as the doughnut finisher. I didn't mind, since far fewer doughnuts were made during a snowstorm. It was actually kind of fun to work during a big weather event like that one. At about 10 o'clock in the morning, a local police chief came into the store and reported that a large tractor-trailer was stuck on the main street hill, just at the bottom of the street below where our store was. Traffic was snarled and no one had much hope of getting the truck up the hill. The street situation was such that there was nowhere for the truck to go. It couldn't go backward and turn around; the nature of the intersection simply didn't permit it. Either the truck went up the hill or it went nowhere. For over six hours, it went nowhere. Every time a police officer would come into the store that day, my dad would signal him back to the kitchen and ask, "Did they get the truck up the hill?"

"Not a chance," one officer replied. My dad graciously volunteered to supply free coffee to those who were working all day in the cold trying to get the truck loose. But all day, the response to the question was the same. The truck remained stuck. I became curious about my dad's curiosity. "Why are you so interested in that truck?" I asked. "Well," he answered, "if they don't have it unstuck by the time we finish here, I'll have to go down and get it unstuck for them."

"What are you talking about?" I replied. "How are *you* going to get it unstuck when every garage and tow truck in town has failed all day long?" My dad just smiled. Because I knew he was an engineer, I didn't doubt that he had a plan. Sure enough, when 4 p.m. rolled around, my dad said, "Let's go free the truck." I was bewildered to see him grab two doughnut screens and take off down the hill.

Well, my dad was certainly confident about his plan. In the midst of the raging blizzard, he went marching down the hill toward the truck carrying two doughnut screens, literally yelling to the other men who surrounded the truck, "Let me try something that I think will work." The men stared in wonder as my dad placed the doughnut screens at the front of each of the back wheels of the huge semi. He commanded the driver to apply the gas pedal. Slowly, the wheels rolled onto the doughnut screens, where they received the traction that they had not been able to get all day long. It was enough to give the truck the momentum it needed to make it to the top of the hill. As several bystanders applauded, my dad picked up his doughnut screens and proudly began to march back to the store. But he stopped when one of the police officers at the bottom of the hill shouted after him. "Mr. Sparks, I need to ask you a question." My dad turned around, smiling, and waited for the inquiry. "Why didn't you come down here at 10 o'clock this morning?"

"Well," my dad paused, "I had to make the doughnuts first." There was a collective groan from the dozen or so men who were still at the bottom of the hill, contemplating what could have been a quick conclusion to their day's labor. I remember feeling a mixture of pride at my dad's solution and guilt that he hadn't gone sooner. Years later, when I was stuck on an icy hill leaving my office at Purdue, I wondered why I hadn't heeded the lesson I had learned from my father: In the winter season, no vehicle should be caught dead without two doughnut screens.

Customers Don't Know What They're Eating

If you're a frequent customer at a doughnut shop, you may want to skip this last section of the chapter. I debated about whether to include this section and I finally decided that people might want to know the truth. Whenever you buy food in a restaurant, you have to entertain the possibility that what you order may not have been prepared quite the way you would prepare it at home. I've thought about this a lot and I've decided that there is simply no way to control the sorts of things that I'm going to tell you about. The only check on these practices is the quality of the people who are preparing the food. It is clear from the preceding chapters that getting a constant supply of quality help was impossible in the doughnut business. That's the reason that I think the things I'm going to tell you are fairly common. That doesn't mean they happen every day. But over a period of months and years, I think they tend to happen in many eating establishments.

I'll start with a rather mild revelation. Several years into our business venture, my dad decided that it would be easier and faster to get doughnuts out on the sales shelves in the morning if he could find a way to preserve the doughnuts from the day before, rather than making a new batch from scratch. His vision led him to experiment with freezing unfinished doughnuts. It didn't work with cake doughnuts at all. But with yeast doughnuts (the ones that would eventually get filled with jelly or topped with frosting), he discovered that with the right thawing procedure, a frozen doughnut was tough to distinguish from a fresh one—at least for a few hours. Consequently, we routinely stocked our doughnut shelves in the morning with frozen yeast doughnuts that had been thawed out. The big negative of this practice is that by noon, these doughnuts were beginning to take on all the qualities of a day-old, stale doughnut. My dad never really wanted to admit it, but for customers who bought a dozen of the freezer doughnuts to take home in the morning, there must have been some intense dissatisfaction upon biting into one of them over a cup of afternoon coffee. I always wondered if we lost more customers on the freezer doughnuts than we gained. Yes, we had fresh doughnuts at 6:30 in the morning, but they were stale by noon.

Freezer doughnuts were the best of the worst. I can't even estimate how many doughnuts fell off the doughnut screens during preparation and hit the floor. The first time this happened while I was working, my impulse was to pick up the fallen doughnut and toss it in the garbage. But over the years of working in the kitchen, I saw the bakers pick up plenty of doughnuts that had fallen on the floor and toss them into the sugar bin to be finished and sold. After a while, this became my standard practice as well. If a doughnut fell on the floor but didn't appear to be any worse off for it, it was usually tossed into the finishing bin with the rest of the batch. In short, many of the "floor" doughnuts ended up becoming "store" doughnuts.

My brother Dale remembers a young woman who was hired to finish the doughnuts and showed up one day with a bad cold. Dale recalls watching in horror as the mucus from her runny nose dropped repeatedly into the large vat of glaze that was used to coat several doughnut varieties. The image is enough to keep me away from a doughnut shop forever. Even though public health departments can do occasional inspections, there is no way to monitor every employee all the time. I think this sort of thing must happen in restaurants more often than people would care to think.

If we found the employees to be uncontrollable when it came to food preparation, we had to admit that sometimes our very own family members were even more uncontrollable. There was one outrageous incident that I didn't learn about until I started talking to my brothers about writing this book. Wayne first told me about it and I didn't believe it. But Garry confirmed the story before I could even bring up the details. I learned from them that my dad was told about it several times over the years and he refused to believe it ever happened. I think he was in defensive denial. He simply couldn't accept the fact that despite his vigilance in making sure that the public received a perfect product, his own sons were contaminating his best efforts. Garry and Wayne are adamant that what I'm about to tell you actually took place. In fact, by Garry's estimate, it happened on at least a half-dozen occasions. I know my brothers well enough not to doubt them when it comes to this sort of memory.

Saturday mornings were generally one of the busiest times in the doughnut shop. More doughnuts were made between 6 a.m. and 1 p.m. on Saturdays than at any other time of the week. At the end of a Saturday morning shift in the kitchen, we were generally ready to take a nap. On a few of these exhausting Saturday mornings, Garry, along with Felipe and his brother Eddy, decided to reward themselves after hours of hard work. One of the last things to be made in the day's doughnut production was a screen of eight apple turnovers. These turnovers were quite sizeable compared to an ordinary doughnut and they involved more labor than most other products we made. According to Garry, Felipe and Eddy decided to experiment. To Garry's amusement and great interest, Felipe and Eddy produced several small vials of strained marijuana from their jacket pockets that hung on the coat hooks in the stockroom just off the kitchen. As they prepared the dough of the apple turnovers, they delicately sprinkled the marijuana into the dough along with the apple filling. When the turnovers were fried, it seems that the THC in the marijuana did a marvelous job of spreading throughout the entire pastry. After the turnovers cooled, Garry, Felipe, and Eddy would stand together back in the kitchen and enjoy what they believed to be the most heavenly bakery product ever made. Apparently, after eating one of the turnovers, they really got a jolt!

When I talked to Garry about the turnovers laced with marijuana, I asked him what happened to the five additional ones after they had cooled. Garry snickered as he told me the horrifying truth: "We just put those out front to sell." My first reaction upon hearing this was to ask him, *"Is it possible that I could have ever eaten one of those turnovers?"* Garry's response was matter-of-fact, with a touch of mischief in his voice: "If you did, you would have known it."

The Main Idea

There is no particular bit of advice in this chapter for the prospective business owner, except this: **In the process of running a business in order to make a livelihood, various experiences will occur that, in the end, shape your life and make your memories.** Part of who I am today consists of the memories made in the doughnut shop. Fortunately, enough of them were interesting, amusing, and bizarre enough to contribute something positive to my personality.

Chapter 10

Life After Doughnuts: Take Time to Do What You Want (But Be Sure You've Prepared for Retirement and Other Life Challenges)

In the spring of 1984, I was completing my first year as an assistant professor in Cleveland. To my surprise, I learned that my parents wanted to visit me with their newly purchased, but previously used, Airstream trailer. In the wake of being put out of work, my father, in the words of Paul Simon's song "Still Crazy After All These Years," chose to "lean on old familiar ways." He decided that he was still a good engineer (he was), and that he could cruise the country in search of short-term jobs for people with his skills. In order to save on meals and lodging, my parents decided to purchase a trailer and travel in a self-contained home. My brothers and I weren't wild about this idea. We thought our parents may actually have been "still crazy after all these years."

As it turned out, there were more short-term engineering jobs than we realized. My parents cruised the Midwest for months and my father worked for numerous companies, receiving surprisingly good compensation. Whenever I talked with them on the phone, they seemed content. I think they enjoyed the adventure of traveling around the country. After all, it was their adventurous personality that propelled their leap into running a doughnut shop 20 years earlier. They hadn't lost that spirit.

Shopping Jobs with an Airstream Trailer, and Another Decision that Produced Regret

In the first few years of trailer life, my parents gradually worked their way west, and my father went back to the same large engineering firm he had worked for before he decided to go for the doughnut life. This assignment went so well that the firm offered my father a permanent job with a retirement account, an excellent salary, and good health insurance. Even though accepting this position would mean a move far away from my brothers and me, as well as an end to their newfound nomadic lifestyle, I enthusiastically encouraged my father to take the position. My brothers agreed.

To our astonishment, our parents decided to keep shopping for short-term jobs and hauling the trailer around the country. While the permanent position was attractive, my father was drawn to the higher hourly wage that most of the short-term jobs offered. It was a decision he'd regret in his senior years when he needed retirement income and didn't have it. I don't know how many times I heard my father kicking himself for the decisions he had made earlier in life that he regarded as handicapping his retirement income. I can still hear my mother's gentle voice seeking to comfort my father and convince him not to be so hard on himself.

The Move Back to Family

After turning down the permanent job, my parents decided to work their way back east and take advantage of the fact that two of my brothers (Wayne and Garry) were living in a large house with their families, on a piece of land that was big enough to accommodate my parents and their trailer. They lived in the trailer on my brothers' land for about a year, and then decided to relocate to an apartment for several reasons. First, my mother was growing tired of living in a trailer. It was cold during the winter and failed to provide a welcoming atmosphere for entertaining guests. Second, the city where my brothers lived wasn't happy about folks living in a trailer that was essentially parked in the driveway. I believe the city actually sent several cease and desist orders to my brothers and threatened them with fines. Third, my father had become accustomed to shopping for engineering jobs and he couldn't curb his habit easily.

He managed to land another engineering job at a firm just north of my brothers' house. The job enabled him to be involved with designing high-tech weapons systems for aircrafts, and was funded by the U.S. government. My father really was a good engineer. I think he even amazed himself at how he was able to go back to these engineering jobs after being away from the trade for so long. He truly loved to design things. During the year he lived in the trailer at my brothers' house, he became intrigued with the idea of building economic housing, and he designed and constructed a dome home made of heavy-duty Styrofoam. It sat on the side of my brothers' driveway, opposite the trailer, and remained there for a long time after my parents moved to their apartment. Eventually, just as the city forced removal of the trailer, they said that the dome home had to go, too. My father occasionally floated his fantasy of actually *living* in the dome home, but my mother emphatically overruled him on that idea.

Family Health Issues

As the post-doughnut years rolled along, age eventually caught up with my parents. My father passed away at age 82 due to complications after heart surgery. While I was not at his bedside when he left us on October 24, 2007, several family members were. I had said goodbye when I visited a few weeks earlier because his condition had worsened. My father had faith in God, and while his passing was a time to mourn our loss, it was also an occasion to remind ourselves of the promise of his eternal destiny and the fact that we would be together again one day. My mother's eyesight was too impaired for her to live alone, so she moved in with my brother Wayne and his wife until she joined my father in eternity on April 7, 2010.

Brother Dale

My oldest brother, Dale, had a distinguished career in law enforcement, with most of his years spent with a state bureau of investigation. He was once mentioned in *Reader's Digest* for his role in solving a high-profile crime. His wife, Nancy, had a distinguished career in her own right as a nurse. She served in hospitals in several states and had certifications in more than one specialty. All of that nursing experience served Dale well when, sadly, he developed early-onset Alzheimer's disease. Nancy elected to care for Dale at home—a task that we recognized as nearly impossible, but we knew Nancy could never be persuaded to do otherwise. She was lovingly dedicated to Dale until he succumbed to this awful disease on April 22, 2016. He was 68 years old.

Brothers Wayne and Garry

Happily, Wayne and Garry are still living. Wayne retired from working as a warden in a state prison system, went to Iraq as a special consultant for their prisons during the war, and returned home to start his own security business that he continues to manage. Garry worked for several years as a parole officer before retiring from the world of law enforcement and taking a job in hospital security, where he currently works.

A Final Reflection

As I revisit this book in March of 2018, I am halfway through my 32nd year as a professor at Purdue University. Earlier in the book, I reflected on some of the ways that the doughnut years prepared me for life as a professor. They also helped prepare me for what I have faced since July 2015—my greatest life challenge to this point. That month, I received an out-of-the-blue medical diagnosis that I had a brain tumor. In the weeks that followed, a biopsy revealed that the tumor was the dreaded glioblastoma—an aggressive brain cancer in which only 5 percent of people survive longer than five years following diagnosis. I learned that this was the same type of tumor that had killed Senator Ted Kennedy as well as Vice President Joe Biden's son Beau. Senator John McCain was also diagnosed with glioblastoma in 2017. My neurologist suggested I retire and go to the beach. Considering the diagnosis I had been given, it wasn't a bad suggestion. But I guess I loved my job too much to consider seriously what would have been a premature retirement. And, like my father, I "tend to lean on old familiar ways." I didn't go to the beach and I didn't retire.

Fortunately, my tumor was operable and I had it removed on August 20, 2015. I had an excellent surgeon who managed to remove almost all of the tumor. But, as often happens in these surgeries, I was left with partial paralysis and weakness on my left side.

In the weeks that followed the surgery, I had the standard postoperative treatment that included more than 40 consecutive days of radiation directed at the surgical area, plus weekly doses of chemotherapy capsules. I tolerated these treatments well. After being discharged from the hospital following surgery, I went to another hospital for physical and occupational therapy to strengthen my left leg and arm. While I was there, my daughter searched the internet for clinical trials to get me follow-up treatment. She found one at Northwestern Memorial Hospital in Chicago that I was able to enter in October 2015. This was an important step to pursue since glioblastoma is particularly aggressive and nearly always returns after tumor removal. My treatment in the clinical trial called for infusions of an immunotherapy drug every three weeks and an MRI scan every nine weeks to see if there was any return of the cancer. So far, I've made it more than two years with clean MRI scans.

Purdue University has been the ideal employer in helping me navigate this challenge. They permitted me to teach online classes for the first semester or two after my surgery. They facilitated my return to the classroom later on by giving me a special parking space near my office and making some structural changes outside and inside my building to make it easier to get around in my power wheelchair, which I need to make my way around campus. I'm a huge fan of Purdue football and basketball, and the folks in the ticket office set me up with special parking and seating to make it easier to get to and from games. I'm able to walk around my house with a cane and I manage to type with only my right hand, although I'm quite a bit slower and I make more errors than I did before my surgery.

The Importance of Prayer, Friends, and Family

During the doughnut shop years, my family faced many challenges, and I learned how to deal with challenges by seeing how my parents handled stress and continued on in the face of adversity. At the urging and support of their pastor, they learned to pray and wait for an answer to come. They also surrounded themselves with a few loyal friends and as many family members as possible. I took these lessons to heart, and they have proven invaluable in responding to my medical situation.

As soon as possible after my diagnosis, I followed the injunction given in the fifth chapter of the book of James in the Bible. Anyone who is sick is instructed to call for the elders of the church and have them pray over him. I contacted my pastor and asked if he could set up such a meeting for me. People in the church responded to this invitation. As I recall, there must have been at least two to three dozen elders gathered in the front of our church's sanctuary to pray for me. It was a very special time. I have held those prayers in my heart and have literally been living on them ever since. I believe in the power of prayer, even though it is difficult to understand exactly what takes place when people seek God's face in that act.

Prayers didn't end with that meeting of the church elders. I've been blessed with a very special group of close friends who pray for me regularly. My name has appeared on prayer lists in churches I've never even seen. Colleagues who I never knew had faith in God have told me they pray for me. I have no doubt that one of the main reasons I have done so well in battling brain cancer is that God has been at work in multiple ways. I believe He has answered prayers by equipping my doctors to deliver great treatment and presiding in His providence over the positive effects of my medications. I don't pretend to understand how all of this works and I make no assumptions about how long I will stay well. Every person eventually dies, notwithstanding prayers for health and life. All I know right now is that I have a strong sense that God, through his Son, Jesus Christ, has granted me more good health over the last few years than I deserve or that the medical community anticipated.

A key ingredient in the equation that has resulted in my good fortune to this point is the incredible support I've received from my wife, Cheri, and my family members. I could not have traveled this road without their prayers and daily support. When I consider trying to write about the many things Cheri has done for me during this chapter of my life, my mind spins. I'll just say that from the time my eyes open each morning to the time they close at night, she is there for me, helping me in whatever way she can. Truly, I could not have chosen to spend my life with anyone who would have been better for me than Cheri—my best friend and the love of my life. My grown children, David, Erin, and Jordan, have each contributed to my joy in life over the past three years in special and unique ways. Not the least of my joys is the incredible grandchildren they have given me—three grandsons (Caleb, Joshua, and Benjamin) and one granddaughter (Autumn).

One of the important lessons I took away from the doughnut years was that family is an extremely important source of strength in facing life's hard times. Close friends are as well. In the final analysis, it proved crucial for my family and me to take this lesson away from the business and to recognize that life isn't over when the business is over. For us, as important as doughnuts were, doughnuts were not everything.

As we reach the end of this part of my story, I'll answer the question I get asked most frequently from people who learn about my journey in a doughnut shop: "Do you still like to eat doughnuts?" My answer is unequivocal. I absolutely still like to eat doughnuts. Glazed ones are my favorite, but I haven't really tasted a doughnut I didn't like. I have continued my interest in doughnuts by launching a fan site on Facebook called "Fans of Rolling in Dough." Anyone can request membership. I post periodic news items about doughnuts on the page; it's amazing how frequently doughnuts appear in the news. If you join the group, I hope you enjoy these posts. Otherwise, I hope you've found this book to be an enjoyable part of the time you spend reading. I'm grateful for the chance to tell you my story.

Chapter 11

Epilogue: You Don't Knead the Dough, the Dough Kneads You

In these final reflections, I want to underscore a point that often escapes business owners and would-be business owners. The general attitude of a person who owns a business is one that takes seriously the task of managing affairs in order to generate revenue and make a living. **What is often lost on an owner or manager is that one doesn't manage a business without being managed by that business as well.** Growing up in a doughnut shop had a tremendous impact on my attitudes about the world, the values I eventually adopted, and the things that I thought were important in life. In this brief epilogue, I attempt to provide an overview of some of the ways this impact happened, and what I took away.

Suspicion

Because one of the biggest battles of the day-to-day operation of the doughnut shop was against people stealing money and supplies, there was constant talk at home about who might be under suspicion and who had definitely been caught. The doughnut shop was even known to be a popular drop-off spot for illegal drugs. The combination of these aspects of the business environment took their toll on our family. All three of my brothers had careers in criminal justice. During the years of the doughnut shop, they saw and heard about plenty of crime. While my brothers took career routes that sought to deal with crime through the criminal justice system, my choice to become a professor may have been shaped by the same dynamic. I simply chose to affect the lives of young people through education—before they got in trouble with the law. Who knows the extent to which our career choices were affected by what we saw in the doughnut business? I suspect that we were affected to a greater extent than we knew. I often have to catch myself today and try to prevent my thinking from leading me to suspect the worst of people's motives. I trace this tendency back to my life in the doughnut shop.

Money

In the doughnut business, money was essential. Each day, we had to depend on customers to keep buying our products. There was a definite orientation to the financial side of the operation. Adding weekly sales figures. Comparing those with figures from the month before, the year before, two years before. Wondering whether prices should be raised. Would we make enough to pay the weekly payroll? Would we have anything left over for savings? These questions were always on my parents' minds. As a result, the doughnut shop experience definitely made an impact on our values. Money was important.

Throughout my adult life, I find myself continuing to think about a big payday in the future. Will I win the lottery? Could I open a new business that earns me millions? Will I win a big payoff from a slot machine while attending an academic conference in Vegas? To a certain extent, everyone may have these thoughts. But I think I have them more than the average person does. I trace this line of thinking back to doughnut days and the constant concern with money. It is a daily obsession that I am happy to be free of in my current work. But the residue has stayed with me and I recognize it.

Hard Work

The impact of the doughnut shop environment was not all negative. I learned from a very young age that hard work paid off. Through my high school and college years, I spent my summers rising at 5 a.m. or earlier to make doughnuts. I worked until I was tired. Then I did it again the next day. There was a profound sense in the doughnut business that there was work to be done each day and that the quality of one's life would depend upon whether the work was done properly. This was a lesson that has served me well to the present day. It helped me get through college with grades good enough to get into graduate school. It helped me succeed in graduate school in the most grueling of moments. And it has helped me earn tenure and promotion to full professor at a major research university. The value of a commitment to hard work should never be underestimated. I am extremely grateful for the environment of the doughnut shop that helped instill this message deep within me. While the dream of a quick payday may have been fostered by the emphasis on money, this was more than offset by the daily realization that we had to work to earn our day's bread.

It Takes All Kinds

Reflecting back on all the advantages of growing up in a doughnut shop, I think perhaps the biggest was that I was able to interact with all kinds of people in a variety of situations. I learned how to serve customers and deal with their complaints. I learned how to make conversation with college professors and lawyers who wanted to talk while they sipped their coffee. I learned how to convince creditors to wait another week for their payments. I learned how to train other people to do the jobs associated with the business. I was also influenced tremendously by some of the people who I met and talked with. In Chapter 3, I mentioned the family pastor who showed up each morning for coffee and a doughnut. The conversations that I had with him during my high school years served as the foundation of my decision to become a Christian—a life-changing choice that continues to shape my daily decisions about how to live. In the final analysis, the years that I spent in the doughnut shop proved to be an education in communication and listening that prepared me well for my academic career and for life in general. I have always been confident in my communication with others and—I hope—relatively easy to talk to.

Internal Locus of Control

There is a concept in psychology called "locus of control." People who have an internal locus of control tend to go through life with the belief that life events depend a great deal on how one personally acts in various situations. In contrast, people who have an external locus of control believe that life events are largely out of their control and happen randomly or chaotically. One thing growing up in a doughnut shop taught me was that how I acted was an important factor in the way things turned out. If I got up late, the whole day's doughnut production went haywire. If I arrived at work on time, the day inevitably went well. In short, I learned the important lesson that I could control my destiny in many circumstances.

One was almost required to learn this lesson in the doughnut business because there seemed to be so many external things that threatened to take control. Success meant learning to cope with these external threats and being able to defy them.

One of the most significant challenges that we faced in the doughnut business came when the state announced a plan to expand the main road that went through town. Our doughnut shop was on that road and we relied on the heavy traffic for our clientele. When the roadwork started, we could not have anticipated the toll it would take on our business. Alternate traffic routes were recommended to daily commuters and the road was torn up for the better part of a year. Business suffered horribly and there was literally nothing that could be done. Many customers told us that they wanted to come to the store, but it was simply too much of a bother to cope with the construction. My parents worried that they would simply run out of cash. At the same time that cash intake was severely disrupted, many of the expenses (franchise fees, rent) remained constant. It always seemed to me that the state should have introduced some program to make financial compensation for this sort of project. We survived the crisis, but barely. Making it through this sort of challenge helped teach us not to give up, that the only answer to external threats was to hold on to every vestige of personal control. One downside to this lesson is that today, I don't do very well in situations where structure is imposed upon me. Perhaps the best example of this happened during my freshman year in college.

I attended a small private college in the Midwest. At the time I enrolled, the college required all male students to enroll in the Reserve Officers' Training Corps (ROTC) program for their freshman year. I knew of this requirement, but I also knew that in my senior year of high school I had obtained a military classification of 4F due to a bleeding ulcer that had hospitalized me for two weeks. I reasoned that if I was unfit for military service, then surely I would not have to go through the ROTC program. During my first week on campus, I visited the ROTC office to get my dismissal from the program. To my horror, I learned that no one was impressed with my 4F classification and didn't really care about it. I was still to report at 6 o'clock on Thursday morning to do drill marches with my platoon. I was outraged. I left the ROTC office and resolved to visit the dean of students. After pouring out my story there, I was politely told that there was no reason I couldn't participate in ROTC. I rehashed my case in the office of the college president. No luck. I was so mad that I called home and threatened to leave the school. I'm glad my parents talked me out of that decision. But I was stuck marching on Thursday mornings all year.

Having already learned that I was in control of my own destiny, I decided that I would show up for the drills with my brass and shoes unpolished. When the drill called for a right face, I would often turn too slowly or even turn in the wrong direction. At the end of the year, I prided myself on the fact that every other male "soldier" had been promoted with a stripe on his sleeve except me. I was making my own statement. I was finding a way to not conform to the structure that was being imposed on me from the outside. Today, I look back on this behavior as somewhat silly and immature. I also recognize that this sort of independence of character that was born in the day-to-day routine of the doughnut business and fueled by my parents' own personalities has served me well in accomplishing the goals I have set in my life.

The Main Idea

The point of this epilogue is perhaps one of the most important: **The experience of going into business will be life-changing.** It will probably be an adventure with both high and low points. If you think you will be the same person after going into business that you were before you went in, then my advice is to do some more research before you start. Because, the fact is, going into business will likely change your life from top to bottom. For some people, this will be great news. For others, it will be a regrettable journey. To the extent that reading my reflections of growing up in the doughnut business might help you decide whether to embark on your own entrepreneurial endeavor, I consider it well worth my efforts to write. If, on the other hand, you have no intention of starting your own business and you have still made it to this page of the book, I trust that something of my story has caught your interest or made you smile. If that's the case, then I am even happier. To cause another to smile is one of my great joys. Perhaps I came to appreciate it as a result of interacting with so many grumpy people who came to our doughnut shop each morning in hopes that a cup of good coffee and a warm doughnut would help them get through their day.

Because I wrote this little collection of memories over a span of many years, it was difficult for me to gain a sense of how others might react when they read it. When some readers told me that they found the overall story to be sad, I was puzzled. But when I went back and read the manuscript all at once, I had more understanding of that response. Without question, the years of running the doughnut shop posed many challenges, stresses, and disappointments. But I would have never endeavored to write of my family's experiences if my predominant reaction to my life in the doughnut business were a sad one. I think one thing the experience gave the whole family was the overwhelming sense that we had a very unique life that few people could match. We enjoyed that. And we enjoyed many other aspects of the life that running the doughnut shop provided. Today, my brothers and I are still a bit nostalgic in thinking back to those years. When my father and mother died, it provided an occasion to drive through the town where the old doughnut shop used to be. We enjoyed reflecting back. I hope you'll agree that even if the tone of many of the stories is on the sad side, you can still appreciate the uniqueness of my family's experience and the many good moments during those 20 years.

A Strange Coincidence Removes Uncertainty About the Book's Title

As I was getting close to the final submission of this manuscript to the publisher, I called an old friend who I asked to do me a favor by reading the draft and offering some constructive feedback. He returned my call early on a Saturday morning when my wife, Cheri, and I were still in bed sipping coffee and watching some TV shows that we had recorded on the DVR. I left the bedroom to take the phone call, and after my friend agreed to read the manuscript, I returned to tell Cheri the reason for the call and to share the good news that someone else would be looking over the text of *Rolling in Dough*. Actually, *Rolling in Dough* was only a working title; I wasn't sure at that point if I would decide to change it. I had a list of several other contenders. As I entered the bedroom and started to give Cheri the update, she instinctively paused the show on the DVR so she could give me her undivided attention. What happened next was truly one of the strangest moments that I can ever remember.

When I finished talking, Cheri hit the "resume play" button on the TV remote and the program that she had been watching (an episode of the prime-time mystery *Bones*) continued. The first words of dialogue that we heard were spoken by one of the female characters in the program. They rang out clearly: "I believe you would say, 'rolling in dough.'" Cheri and I looked at each other in disbelief. We were both convinced that our hearing had been mistaken. Cheri rewound the DVR and we played the dialogue again. We had heard the words correctly. The character who had spoken these words was trying to explain to her partner what it meant for someone to be "flush." After rewinding the DVR several more times and listening repeatedly to the words "rolling in dough," my statistical training from graduate school started to take over. This manuscript had been tentatively named *Rolling in Dough* several years earlier. What was the probability that Cheri would have been watching a TV show that contained this expression in it? How about the probability that she would have also been watching this program at the exact moment that I got a phone call about the book? How about the further probability that she would have stopped the DVR just before this line of dialogue? I don't know how to begin to compute the probability that all of these things would have happened together. I do know from reading statistical theory that amazing coincidences like this one do happen more frequently than most people imagine. I also know that picking out these incidents after they happen instead of predicting them beforehand is sometimes referred to as the "selection fallacy." Nevertheless, I also know that when one experiences a coincidence like this, it can seem like much more than a mere coincidence. I never thought about changing the title of the book after this incident.

When I told this story to one of my friends who is a pastor of a large church, he reflected for a moment and said, "This is surely a sign. The trouble is I don't know exactly what sort of a sign it is." The fact that you are reading these words means that I decided to go ahead and publish the book. After this mysterious experience with the words "rolling in dough," I felt compelled to move the project ahead. I hope most readers will be happy that I did. I'm still trying to decide if the episode of *Bones* had any cosmic significance beyond the fact that it was a truly amazing coincidence.

ABOUT THE AUTHOR

Glenn Sparks is a professor of communication. When he was a child, his parents opened a doughnut franchise and twenty years later, Glenn had handled over 8 million doughnuts. He credits his experiences in the doughnut shop for helping him to foster the skills he needed later in life to publish academic articles, explain scientific findings to the press, teach undergraduates effectively, and write a popular text book that college students would enjoy reading. He also drew upon his experiences to help raise three children and stay married for 36 years (and still going). His unusual hobby of playing the theremin is probably unrelated to his years in the doughnut shop. He lives in Indiana with his wife Cheri.